RUMBLE IN THE JUNGLE RELOADED

NAVIGATING BUSINESS ON THE AFRICAN CONTINENT

RUTENDO HWINDINGWI

"Rutendo has a rare depth of experience in providing sound, grounded advice to companies that are doing business on the African continent. He's written this book at a time when it's clear that Africa is the frontier for investing in emerging markets – and it's a must-read for anyone who wants to understand the nuances of doing business in Africa."
– Stephen Tio Kauma, Director and global head of human resources at Afreximbank

"Rutendo is a shining light of energy, knowledge and optimism on all things Africa, and a connector of people and ideas. Read and enjoy!"
– Lee Dawes, CEO of GE Steam Power Africa and president of the American Chamber of Commerce in South Africa

"The success of the opportunities in Africa depends on empowering its greatest asset – its people. Rutendo illustrates this beautifully in this book."
– George Land, Senior vice president and head of business strategy and operations at NBA Africa

"Africa has a uniqueness that's a healthy mixture of challenge and opportunity, which Rutendo brings out so well in this book."
Mel Brooks, Regional CEO for Africa
and Middle East at G4S

"Until you have lived in, worked in, and fully immersed yourself in Africa, you cannot begin to understand her. Dr Rutendo Hwindingwi, a passionate African citizen and African realist, shares his beautifully written perceptions into this continent, providing insights on uncovering the abundant business opportunities for those who are willing to step outside of their comfort zone. Not your typical business book!"
– Angela Russell, CEO of the American Chamber of Commerce in South Africa

"To define its own destiny, Africa needs to shape its own 'jungle'. *Rumble In The Jungle Reloaded* is a remarkable read highlighting this."
– Dr Shiferaw Teklemariam, Former Ethiopian ambassador to South Africa

"Rutendo is an incredibly enthusiastic supporter of promoting business in Africa. His anecdotes, insights and experiences make for great reading. Originating from a failed state in the region, Rutendo knows first-hand what makes economies fail – and also what makes them work."
– Dr Martyn Davies, MD for emerging markets and Africa at Deloitte

"Rutendo's commitment to and personal passion for Africa shine through in this book, which is as dynamic as he is himself. Africa is the water and rushing rivers, and business is the land, not the other way around. Mould to it or be washed away – that's his key message, based on years of lived experience in senior management in multinationals and chambers of commerce."
– Jon Foster-Pedley, Dean and director of Henley Business School, Africa

"In this book, Rutendo describes a continent at a crossroads – dealing with her past while simultaneously facing uncertainty in a fast-changing world. Africa has all she needs to succeed, but she'll need to better leverage three critical factors: people, people and people."
– Dr Jackie Chimhanzi, CEO of the African Leadership Institute

"Enjoy *Rumble In The Jungle Reloaded* as it delightfully guides you in understanding this wonderful continent better."
– David Hamadziripi, Zimbabwean ambassador to South Africa

"*Rumble In The Jungle Reloaded* is engaging, enjoyable and insightful – a pragmatic reach-for guide for anyone looking to do business in Africa."
– Wesley Ekman, Global sales director at Coats Digital

"Cultural sensitivity, global mindfulness and geopolitical awareness are all qualities that help us work, live and navigate across borders. These qualities are especially critical when doing business, leveraging opportunities and managing multifaceted relationships in Africa. With real-life examples, a keen eye for detail and a gift for educating his readers, Dr Rutendo Hwindingwi offers clear guidance and thought-provoking advice to meet the challenges and prospects of this amazing continent."

– Ruth Lockwood, Head of strategic sales for South East Asia (and former commercial director for Africa) at Santa Fe Relocation

"I have known and worked with Dr Rutendo Hwindingwi for several years. His intellect and engaging personality, along with his energy and lived experience on the continent, make him a compelling expert in this field. The book, artfully, uses metaphor, history and fact to articulate the challenges and excitement experienced when engaging in the African opportunity – a must-read for those wishing to do business on the continent."
– Leon Ayo, CEO of Warwick Consulting EMEA
and president of the British Chamber of Business
in Southern Africa

"Rutendo shows us that Africa will never be free unless it owns and controls its own wealth, and comes up with homegrown solutions to its challenges – something that is close to my heart."
– Dr Frank Aswani, CEO of the African Venture
Philanthropy Alliance

Published by Mercury
an imprint of Burnet Media

•

Burnet Media is the publisher of Mercury and Two Dogs books
info@burnetmedia.co.za
www.burnetmedia.co.za

PO Box 53557, Kenilworth, 7745, South Africa

•

First published 2022
1 3 5 7 9 8 6 4 2

•

Publication © 2022 Burnet Media
Text © 2022 Rutendo Hwindingwi

•

Front and Back cover photography
© Tinashe Hwindingwi: thwindingwi@gmail.com

•

•

Distributed by Jacana Media
www.jacana.co.za

•

Printed and bound by Shumani RSA
www.shumanimills.co.za

•

ISBN 9781990956454

Set in Minion Pro 11pt

To my wife P and my sons Joshua, Nathan and Arnold

ABOUT THE AUTHOR

Born in the eastern part of Zimbabwe, Dr Rutendo Hwindingwi sees himself as an "African realist", applying a healthy blend of optimism and realism when it comes to developing business on the African continent. Having advised and structured business development programmes for multinational companies in more than 20 African countries for more than 20 years, Rutendo has intimate knowledge of how to build a business development strategy and guide it through Africa's complex business terrain.

He is the African regional director for Elev8, a multinational focused on global digital skilling and transformative education initiatives for enterprises and governments; as well a non-executive director for the British Chamber of Business in

Southern Africa and chairman of the American Chamber of Commerce in South Africa, which represent MNCs from their respective countries' operations in Africa.

Prior to joining Elev8, he was an associate director at Deloitte Africa. As founding faculty and programme director, he was instrumental in the formation of Alchemy by Deloitte, which offered customised executive leadership programmes on the back of Deloitte's global advisory practice. Before that, Rutendo was the divisional director for Sage in the Africa, Middle East and Australasia office. His primary focus was growing the footprint of Sage as a leading business management software vendor for small and medium-to-large enterprises across the continent through its client and channel networks.

Rutendo holds a PhD in International Business Strategy from the University of the Witwatersrand, an MSc in strategic management from Derby University in the UK, and a diploma in executive business leadership from the Zimbabwe Institute of Management. He is happily married to his wife "P"; they have three teenage sons, Joshua, Nathan and Arnold.

CONTENTS

PROLOGUE
WELCOME TO ZAIRE

"The jungle is stronger than the elephant."
African proverb

The year was 1974; the location Kinshasa, Zaire.

For several weeks, the eyes of the world had been on this exotic, impenetrable country smack-bang in the heart of Africa; a place of forbidden history and untapped bounty. But its focus was not on the geopolitical value of a land overflowing with precious raw minerals, or even the cultural and socioeconomic interest of a young independent state. What the world wanted to see was a fight – a boxing match between the reigning world heavyweight champion, George Foreman, and probably the most famous man in the world at the time, Muhammad Ali.[1] This was the Rumble in the Jungle – a fight so unique, so charged with passion and intrigue, that nearly half a century later it is still described as "the most intoxicating bout in boxing history".[2]

Ali and Foreman were in Zaire at the invitation of its president, Mobutu Sese Seko, a leader in the process of entrenching himself as one of the definitive strongmen of post-colonial Africa. He had changed his country's name from Republic of the Congo in 1971, and his own name from Joseph Mobutu in 1972. Now he had offered a $10-million purse to boxing promoter Don King for the rights to host the world heavyweight title fight at Stade du 20 Mai in Kinshasa.

Africa had never hosted a fight of this calibre before. Nor has it since. Perceived as just another backward nation lost in the vast "Dark Continent", Zaire – one of many newly independent African nations – was at the time largely invisible to the rest of the world. It was thus a curious and unexpected host for a world heavyweight title fight. Although it was a growing economic hub in the region, strategically positioned and abundant in natural resources, it lacked modern conveniences and the well-heeled crowds of Western countries, and Mobutu ruled it with an iron fist. But $10 million was a substantial amount of money back then, and we need not spend time mulling over the choice of venue. What is relevant is the role the venue played in deciding the outcome.

George Foreman was the world number one, with a 40-0 record in professional boxing, including 37 knockouts. He was younger and stronger than Muhammad Ali, and was expected to win the fight hands-down. For the purposes of this book, Foreman represents the Market Leader, the equivalent of an established multinational company (MNC) that wants to increase its footprint on African soil. Typically, such an MNC would have a history in mostly developed markets, but it would believe that its strategies were "tried and tested", with little left to learn about accessing new markets, African or otherwise. Such was the case of George Foreman, who believed he had won the fight before it had even begun.

In this story, Muhammad Ali represents the underdog. A previous champion, regarded as something of a spent force, he was trying to claw his way back to the top after being stripped of his title eight years earlier for refusing the Vietnam War draft. Tellingly, Foreman had knocked out, within two rounds, both Joe Frazier and Ken Norton, the only two fighters to have beaten Ali, and there were genuine fears that he might do Ali some serious damage.

Although both fighters were African-American, neither had been to Zaire before. As we shall see in the pages to come, the way they adapted to their unfamiliar surroundings, and the strategies they adopted both before and during the fight, would have direct bearing on the outcome. The end result was a boxing match that would go entirely beyond the ordinary: unusual location, unusual culture, unusual politics, unusual economics, unusual climate, unusual people, even unusual timing – the bout was scheduled for 4am local time to optimise television viewership in the US. From this unique mixing pot came one of the greatest fights of all time, a standout world event contested in the "jungles" of Africa, and broadcast to more than 100 countries and a quarter of the world's population amounting to one billion people.

As history well knows, in eight gruelling rounds it was the underdog, Ali, who prevailed.

According to Ali's biographer, Thomas Hauser, the Rumble in the Jungle "inspired more global joy than any athletic achievement in history".[3] We might expand on that to say there is much joy to be had in Africa – and indeed much success. For Ali, the fight in Kinshasa was a precious opportunity for redemption. In adapting to the unique challenges of the "jungle" with more savvy and foresight than Foreman, he gave himself the best chance of success.

Today, far more so than in the 1970s, Africa is a continent awash with opportunity – but it has a unique way of doing business and it often doesn't operate according to global corporate norms.

Those who understand and adapt to it will – like Muhammad Ali – be more likely to win.

AFRICA, LAND OF CRISIS AND OPPORTUNITY

"What is past is gone, what is hoped for is absent; for you is the hour in which you are."
African proverb

A business journalist once asked what I meant when I called myself an "African realist". The question allowed me to reflect on my role in business on this continent. The label, which I created myself, comes out of a healthy blend of optimism and reality. Almost daily I work with individuals and organisations from vastly different backgrounds with the purpose of positioning Africa as "open for business".

Although I love it and would not swap it for anything, it's no easy task, because African challenges can seem insurmountable. I continually draw hope from my surroundings – and one source of hope, fittingly, comes from the wild. I have a talk called "The Hyena Effect", which looks at team dynamics and leadership development. In it, I compare the hunting success rate of a lion – which, when the animal hunts alone is unlikely to top 20%, increasing to about 30% for hunts in pairs or groups[1] – with that of a hyena, whose pack-hunting success rate can be as high as 74% (though lone hunters are far less successful).[2] And let's not forget about African wild dogs: with an impressive 80% success rate, they are among Africa's most effective predators.[3] Who would have thought that the stats would favour these animals over the king of the jungle?

The main reason hyena and wild dogs are more successful is that they both generally hunt in packs – team work! – and they chase their prey relentlessly over long distances – persistence! Team work and persistence are what encourage me as an African realist: when the chips are down, I remember the truly African spirit of Ubuntu (more on this later) and remind myself to hang on – success will come.

In other words: never give up... but when you do, start again!

Africa is indeed "open for business". The continent as a whole faces immense challenges, but it is a place of abundant gifts, of deep and authentic humanity, and of unparalleled opportunity. They say that Africa changes a person – so the question is not whether Africa is ready for you, but if your "Grow Africa" strategy is ready for Africa.

* * *

Yes, Africa is a continent in flux. It is a place of historical impediments so overwhelming that it remains dramatically underdeveloped compared to much of the rest of the world. And yet it is a place that many feel represents the last great opportunity on the planet for growth and development – particularly since, according to *The Economist*, 25% of the world's population will be African by 2050.[4]

While Africa still grapples with the detritus of genocide, slavery, racism, colonialism and apartheid, its people have never been more connected to and aware of the global economy. They have never lived at a time when technological advances have such scalable and profoundly positive potential, or in a more ethically aware age where their voices count for something (although there is, of course, much progress to be made). And as their numbers increase, they have never offered such market potential.

Herein lies the African conundrum.

How can Africa's people – and those doing business with Africa's people – overcome the continent's considerable challenges to take advantage of today's gilt-edged opportunities?

This state of opportunity may exist for only a fleeting moment, and the stakes are high: it is a chance to eliminate remnants of a history that has impeded Africa's progress thus far. I believe that success in business provides the roadmap to a brighter future.

What is it about Africa that makes it such a cauldron of discussion and debate?

From the monumental pyramids of Egypt, through the scorching Sahara and the equatorial jungles of the Congo, among the valleys and mountains that form the foundation of human civilisation in the Great Rift Valley, across plains of teeming wildlife to the ruins of Great Zimbabwe and the cold-water shores of the Cape of Good Hope, many wars have been fought on this continent and much blood has been spilled. Humans have been traded as chattel, children abducted, villages ravaged. Dictators and warlords have wrought destruction, clinging to power while plundering state resources. Drums have echoed from mountaintops, volcanoes have erupted and the earth has trembled… So Africans may be excused for peeping in the rear-view mirror as they reach for a more prosperous and equitable future.

Looking at the continent's long history of conflict and tragedy, we may consider that such cataclysmic eruptions of fear, despair, excitement and exasperation would not occur where there is no value; that even in the face of rampant poaching, Africa's fauna has flourished and abundant flora has carpeted its landscapes.

Because Africa *is* hope.

As the proverb that begins this chapter suggests, it is only in the present that we can change the future. I look at my children and think of their children's children, and the reality grips me: the Africa of the past will not be the Africa of tomorrow.

Today's Millennials seek to radically change the way we think, do business and treat the Earth. They are closely followed by Generation Z, a demographic cohort uniquely defined as the first to be brought up on a diet of the internet and intimately familiar with technology and social media. At the same time, we are seeing world leaders traversing Africa, seeking stronger relationships intended to drive development.

The late Bahamian preacher and leadership consultant Myles Munroe said, "The greatest tragedy in life is not death, but a life without purpose." I believe the time has come when we African people are ready to acknowledge that a large part of resolving our challenges and capitalising on the continent's opportunities is the realisation of our united purpose as individuals. In doing so, we will become more powerful and more integrated into the global family.

Those companies and organisations willing to contribute to that purpose have so much potential in the years ahead. Multinational companies (MNCs) in particular will play a key role as they invest in countries where they see opportunities for growth. But to successfully expand their business-development strategy in Africa, it is becoming increasingly critical that they understand the fabric of the continent.

Let's look at some figures.

The population of Africa is currently around 1.3 billion. The African Development Bank estimates that by 2050 it will have increased to 2.4 billion.[5] It is estimated that GDP growth rate at that time will be 5.3%, compared to a rate of approximately 4% in 2021 for sub-Saharan Africa.[6] (These estimates pre-date the Covid-19 pandemic, the long-term economic ramifications of which remain to be seen.) The potential market is, therefore, an obvious attraction – but this future comes with its own challenges.

On the one hand, Africa has a large and rapidly growing population. On the other, it is estimated that 18% are unemployed, compared to a global average of 7.5%. Africa has a youthful population, keen to engage with new technology and opportunities in robotics, artificial intelligence, virtual reality and blockchain. But the long-running problems of corruption and poor leadership, combined with poor health conditions, present significant hurdles for these young people. Sometimes it is truly difficult to imagine enough leaders on this continent, with its melting pot of culture, commerce and corruption, successfully delivering consistent growth and elevating the quality of life of its people. And yet, the potential for rapid development and economic progress is undeniable.

Consider the significant shifts that have taken place globally in the last few years. The controversy of Brexit has continued to play out in Europe; the US and China have become increasingly mired in a new Cold War; the Covid-19 pandemic has claimed millions of lives; and the Russian invasion of Ukraine has ushered in a new period of geopolitical instability. All have far-reaching implications, and all are set against a backdrop of rising inequality and environmental concerns. It is undeniable that the developed world has numerous challenges of its own, many on a global scale.

Europe, Asia and North America are all, in one way or another, trying to strengthen their ties in Africa. For example, China has lent hundreds of billions of dollars to various African countries as part of its Belt and Road Initiative. In response, leaders of the G7 nations announced in June 2022 a US$600-billion lending initiative for developing countries, with a particular focus on Africa. Interested MNCs may be of African origin or from more developed economies abroad. For them, Africa offers a trove of opportunity: vast populations to uplift from poverty and turn into powerful new markets, as has happened in Southeast Asia. They know that, despite its challenges, the continent offers one last great opportunity for growth, and that there is real reason to believe that Africa could be front-footed in helping to develop global solutions.

INTRODUCTION

Rumble In The Jungle Reloaded provides a broad roadmap for successfully navigating the African business landscape. It does so by looking at five fundamental lessons I have gleaned from the famous Rumble in the Jungle clash between Muhammad Ali and George Foreman. These key lessons are:

- Understand the territory
- Innovate
- Know your threats
- Grab opportunities
- Apply relentless drive and determination

Combining these insights with my own corporate experience in more than 20 African countries over two decades, I will help to unravel the mysteries and magnificence of Africa, and present the tools required to access its wonder, strength and potential.

* * *

Having lived most of my life in Africa, I have come to the conclusion that it is impossible for anyone in business or politics to "sum up" the continent in terms of its people, resources and landscapes. It's like looking at the stars and seeing their beauty and wonder, but being overcome by the complexity of it all.

Africa is a densely packed continent of 54 independent countries. That means 54 governments, 54 heads of state, 54 economies and countless cultures and ethnicities all jostling for a place in the sun. Africa's strength – often consciously ignored – lies in its grand diversity. Any entrepreneur or established business or organisation that wants to expand into and flourish in Africa needs to understand that diversity is in its very DNA.

The late Muammar Gaddafi, leader of Libya, was known for his dream of wanting to create a United States of Africa. Whether his motives were benign or malign, more than a decade after his death that idea is still but a dream. I have often reflected on the concept of unification. The efforts of the African Union, the Southern African Development Community (SADC) and the Economic Community of West African States (ECOWAS) have been underwhelming on the whole, especially when it comes to facilitating change on the continent. That raises the question: is Africa's strength to be found in creating a façade of homogeneity – or will it flourish through the power of its diversity? My vote is for the latter.

When people asked me about the opportunities in Africa, I used to struggle to adequately and truthfully explain the status quo, the reality of Africa. I might have talked about the diamond-rich DRC in the context of "blood diamond wars", misappropriated wealth at the expense of citizens and the destruction of a nation. Or the oil wealth of Angola and Nigeria, and the tragedy of so much of it being lost – processed abroad rather than in local refineries as a way to secure continental resources. Or the booming tourism opportunities in North Africa and its exotic World Heritage sites, like the Great Pyramid of Giza and the Nile River, which were overshadowed by the Arab Spring uprisings and ongoing terrorism that obstructs real progress.

When faced with the question of opportunity today, I find that my response has changed. Africa's opportunities, I believe, are in the very problems that seem to be holding back its progress. When you look at the African continent from this perspective, everything turns upside down. The colonial view was that Africa was a repository of natural resources to be exploited at will, despite the challenges. The new vision is that of a place of many people with many eminently solvable challenges that will unlock markets and growth. And yes, part of Africa's deal are the natural resources and innate wealth embedded in this earth that have been here since creation.

This inversion presents a heightened sense of opportunity, of what can be achieved.

There is a special connection Africans have with their origins that goes beyond the comprehension of the mind and cannot be measured by the eye. It permeates the soul of every African; a unique imprint that has remained with us through the aeons. It is reflected in a colourful and vibrant cascade of cultures, history and tribes – and whether we are Arabs in Algeria, Buganda in Uganda, Akan in Ivory Coast, Maasai in Kenya or any other people of Africa, we have in the past put so much effort into trying to differentiate ourselves that we have sometimes overlooked our deeper heritage. And we have often forgotten that most of the world sees Africans as one people anyway.

I have come to realise that I can combine my personal identity with one on a continental scale. I was not just fortunate to be born on this continent, I was blessed! This is not in any way a denigration of other people or cultures around the world; it is an affirmation of the modern African identity, a reality and a privilege of which I am immensely proud.

Being able to tap into that African-ness is the key to success on this continent.

When I write about Africa, it's not as some imaginary, faraway place, so often misconstrued in the global media as a dark pit of despair and suffering. When I write about Africa, I am writing about home. I write from the perspective of a personal culture forged in the flames of many cultures and ethnicities. My love for this continent is not blurred by a veil of mystery and misconception; it is built on a deep understanding of its incredible possibilities, which are centred around its people, its vibrancy and, above all else, its potential.

I am an "African realist". I believe that for a business looking for opportunity in the years ahead, there is no better place than the continent I call home. Africa really is the next Big Thing. And so, as you prepare to embark on your journey through this book, I welcome you to my home, and the home of a billion-plus fellow Africans. Taking words, perhaps surprisingly, from a Standard Bank advertisement from some years ago:

"They call it Africa; we call it Home."

UNDERSTAND THE TERRITORY

*"Where water is the boss,
there the land must obey."*
African proverb

The fight: Rumble in the Jungle

The Rumble in the Jungle was Africa's first heavyweight championship match. Looking to draw attention to Zaire's great beauty and vast natural resources, the government staged and hosted the match – then-President Mobutu Sese Seko personally paid each of the fighters US$5-million simply for showing up.

The bout's title, "Rumble in the Jungle", was given by US boxing promoter Don King. It had initially been tagged "From the Slave Ship to the Championship!" but when Mobutu Sese Seko heard about that, he ordered all posters bearing those words to be burnt.

> Ali agreed. "I wanted to establish a relationship between American blacks and Africans," he wrote later. "The fight was about racial problems, Vietnam. All of that." He added: "The Rumble in the Jungle was a fight that made the whole country more conscious."[1]

Of course, Ali himself was no stranger to controversy. He had ruffled more than a few American feathers by converting to Islam and dodging service in the military. But "in Africa he was beloved. For a nation that had just won its independence from Western powers, Ali's bold stance against the American military industrial complex spoke volumes."[2]

In the days leading up to the bout, media reports highlighted the fact that Ali had flown into the country earlier than Foreman, and had spent more time getting to know the culture and the people of Zaire. Unlike Foreman, Ali had moved into a villa on the banks of the Zaire River, and interacted with the people on his jogs through the neighbourhood.

"Ali was out often in the community, taking long daily runs and allowing visitors to watch him train – and listen to him talk. While Foreman was reticent, Ali was Ali, never at a loss for words." [3]

In contrast, and rather unfortunately for him, it is reported that Foreman came "to Africa with his German Shepherd, the same kind of dog the Belgians had used to keep the populace in line. That started him on the wrong foot with the people of Zaire. Not that Foreman stood much of a chance to begin with."[4]

Neither Ali nor Foreman had been to Zaire before – the climate, culture and people were new and different to both of them. The way in which Ali adapted to and engaged with Zaire's conditions and citizens gave him a significant advantage over his seemingly unbeatable opponent. Before the fight had even begun, the "Market Leader" had lost market share to the "underdog".

The fight had been scheduled for the very early morning in Zaire, to make for prime-time viewing in the US. At 4.30am on 30 October 1974, local spectators gathered under the light of the moon at the outdoor Stade du 20 Mai.

They were chanting "*Ali, bomaye*" – "Ali, kill him".

Round 1: Understanding the territory

I have had the privilege of working in a number of countries in Africa. My successes and failures have enriched me, and provided valuable experience and insight through first-hand experience of how to be successful in this vast and dynamic market – a market unlike any other.

Take developed markets like Japan, the US, the UK or Europe. There is no great mystery in accessing these tried-and-tested markets, each of which, from a business and marketing perspective, is relatively homogeneous. Not so Africa! There is no other place on the planet with so much cultural, tribal and linguistic diversity, nor such a concentration of countries in one land mass. Over the centuries, Africa has been divided on the basis of religion (Christian, Muslim, African traditional), as colonies (Lusophone, Anglophone, Francophone) and according to ethnic groups numbering in the thousands. None of these identities tells the individual story of Africa, yet all are now part of Africa's DNA. Added to that is the fact that change in Africa is being accelerated by digitisation and the new global environmental, social and governance (ESG) demands.

To grasp the scale of Africa's diversity, it is helpful to note that its populations, groups and languages exceed those of North and South America combined, while being condensed into an area roughly three-quarters the size – as seen in Table 1 below.

	Africa	North and South America
Number of countries	54[5]	52
Land size	30.37-million square kilometres[6]	42.08-million square kilometres[7]
Population	1.3-billion	1-billion
Languages	2,000[8]	1,000[9,10]
People groups	3,713	2,451

Table 1: Continental comparison of Africa versus North and South America combined 2019/2020 [11]

The sheer size of the continent, its diversity and its cauldron of cultural, linguistic and regional complexities are what sets Africa apart. This diversity, combined with a rapidly growing population, presents formidable and complex challenges – and creates a significant barrier to entry for entrepreneurs. With Africa still bearing the scars of colonialism, slavery, civil war, disease and epidemics, it may appear almost impossible to conquer this territory. But as the African saying goes, "How does one eat an elephant? One bite at a time."

Realising that territories are unique and constantly changing, and then adapting accordingly, is key. And in the post-pandemic world, being adaptable to unique conditions is more relevant than ever. Many companies and entrepreneurs fail in Africa because they do not take the time to understand the dynamics of the specific countries in which they want to operate – they're not prepared to work bite by bite. Sometimes it's because of ignorance, but mostly it's because of arrogance, preconceived ideas or an unwillingness to understand the territory. That said, we need not be under the misapprehension that African solutions necessarily have to *originate* in Africa. Neither do they need only a black pedigree. Indeed, with the globalisation of societies and economies, its solutions could just as well be conceptualised in China and tested in Australia!

When we think of overcoming Africa's complex challenges, it is worth remembering how Muhammad Ali won the hearts and minds of the people of Zaire: by spending time with them and trying to understand their culture.

"It isn't the mountains ahead to climb that wear you out; it's the pebble in your shoe."
Muhammad Ali

Case study 1.1: M-Pesa in South Africa?

You might be familiar with the story of M-Pesa, the mobile banking app launched in 2006 that has had extraordinary success in Kenya through a link between Vodacom and its local Kenya subsidiary Safaricom. In December 2018,[12] an average of more than 500 transactions were processed every second,[13] and in the fiscal year 2019, 37-million active customers carried out more than 11-billion transactions.

This model has made waves not only in Africa but worldwide. A less well-known story is how Vodacom, whose majority shareholder is Vodafone Plc (UK), tried to launch M-Pesa in South Africa, where it is headquartered and where it has had tremendous success in the mobile phone network space.

According to *Fin24 Tech*,[14] when M-Pesa first launched in South Africa in 2010, Vodacom's target was 10-million local users; in Kenya, mobile network Safaricom had more than 11-million M-Pesa users. South African users were dramatically short of that, and by May 2016 Vodacom announced that it was pulling the plug on M-Pesa in South Africa due to its poor performance.

One might have expected that M-Pesa and the South African market were a match made in heaven. South Africa had a bigger population and a stronger economy than Kenya, and Vodacom was established there, as it was in Kenya. But from reports at the time, five key reasons[15] can be seen to have contributed to the failure of M-Pesa in South Africa:

1. In Kenya, the number of people without access to financial services, especially in rural areas, was far larger than in South Africa. M-Pesa thus became the first link not just to technology (via mobile phones) but also to formal financial transactions for a group that had previously not been catered for.

2. Unlike in Kenya, where Safaricom was the sole telecoms player, in South Africa there were already several large players, including MTN, Cell C and Telkom. With Safaricom's large market share, it was easier to reach the critical mass of users.

3. In South Africa, Vodacom's banking partner was Nedbank, which does not enjoy a reputation as a people's bank and is seen more as a bank that targets the elite.

4. The banking rules and regulations in South Africa are stricter than in Kenya, whose regulators did not consider M-Pesa a banking solution. It thus avoided the central bank's red tape, which was not the case in South Africa.

5. Kenyan leadership understood the requirements of the unbanked in their country, whereas judgment at a high level in South Africa was clouded.

It is so important for MNCs to understand the nuances of each country and territory. To summarise the M-Pesa story in Africa: same product, same company, different countries, different outcomes.

Having worked for MNCs for more than 20 years, I can't claim that I have not been guilty of making similar mistakes. But hindsight is the perfect science;

hopefully we can avoid such mistakes in the future. As in this case, gaining better insight into the specifics of a territory is absolutely key.

Personal experience: Hustling in Zimbabwe

The year was 2005 and Zimbabwe's economy was beginning to face the brunt of the badly implemented land-reform programme of the late 1990s. Previously, the country's booming economy had led to its being nicknamed the "breadbasket of Africa". With a diversified economy that included an agricultural base and strong food exports from the region, Zimbabwe had once been destined to become a leading economy under the leadership of president Robert Mugabe – seen in Africa as a liberation hero, and highly respected worldwide for his intellect and political leadership, both of which attracted investment.

The impact on the economy of the failed land-reform policies was, however, significant. In 2005, industrial output was on average 15% of GDP, against a peak of 25% in the early 1990s.[16] Coupled with the downturn in manufacturing, this translated into weak exports. The inflation rate was a crippling

586%[17] and foreign currency was in limited supply.

This dire set of circumstances, fuelled by the shortage of foreign currency, led to the emergence of a thriving black market, or "parallel market". The currency freefall that followed led to the crash of the Zimbabwe dollar against the US$ exchange rate to an official Reserve Bank level of 1:36,000! On the black market, for the same currency, it was almost 1:50,000 – a difference of 36%.[18] At that point, if the economy of Zimbabwe were a patient in a hospital, it would have been in ICU!

At the time, I was working as a general manager for an SME called Chips Computing Services, which sold and implemented Sage business-management software solutions to a number of medium to large corporates in the country. It was a small, family-owned business that was operating quite well with close to 50 staff, including subcontracted consultants. We boasted about 300 clients that were on the Zimbabwe Stock Exchange (ZSE), and that were benefiting from our services in one way or the other. Chips Computing Services was also the distributor of our software in Zimbabwe, and we competed as a reseller globally, with distributors in Africa, the Middle East and Australasia.

One of our major challenges was purchasing our stock-in-trade software in foreign currency from the principal headquartered in Europe and, regionally, in South Africa. Despite being a small firm, and even under such harsh economic conditions, we were able to trump our international competitors in the region, and rose to become one of the top-performing resellers for our software brand on a global scale.

How did we achieve this against such adverse conditions in a small market? We did it by understanding our territory and adjusting our strategy accordingly. Among a multitude of smaller interventions, two main actions contributed to our success.

First, we realised that we had a unique advantage, in that a significant number of our clients were listed on the local bourse. We were able to convince our principal in Europe and South Africa of the strategic advantage of maintaining these clients for the long term. With our excellent record of achievement in Zimbabwe, we were able to negotiate an unbelievably soft credit arrangement with our principals. This not only made a significant positive impact on our cash flow, it also allowed us to grow market share, as other local distributors were not able to secure similar arrangements with their vendors.

Second, we intentionally targeted companies that were exporters, because they were paid in forex. Consequently, we were in a better position to pay for our software and services, and were better able to remit to our principals.

It sounds really simple, but when you are operating in an aggressively hyperinflationary environment that is also going through political turmoil, such leverage was crucial to surviving and thriving.

Even though 2005 was bad in Zimbabwe, by 2008 things were much, *much* worse. But even as inflation hit a catastrophic 231,000,000%[19], Chips continued to perform beyond expectation because it took the prevailing realities of the environment seriously.

Hyperinflation
2008 was the worst year I lived in Zim. There was no food in shops, hyperinflation was crazy, people used to go to the bakery to wait in queues for bread (I even ate bread that had a metal nail in it), we didn't go to school for more than half a year... never again #Zimbabwe[20]

– Tweet

Case study 1.2:
Navigating South Africa's territory

In South Africa, where I am based now, I look at the challenges that confront current president Cyril Ramaphosa. He has committed to the land-reform programme, without which it would be difficult for him to maintain the support, itself significantly eroded, of the grassroots majority his party captured in the 2019 elections.

Looking at the country's population demographics alongside data about farmland and agricultural ownership in Table 2 below, it is easy to see that a sociopolitical and economic dilemma confronts the country's president.

Racial grouping	Population demographics	Farmland and agricultural ownership[21]
Black	80.2%	4%
Coloured	8.8%	15%
White	8.4%	72%
Indian/Asian	2.5%	5%
"Other" (and land co-owners)		4%

Table 2: South Africa's population demographics versus farmland and agricultural ownership

In addition to the challenge of the basic means of production being in the hands of the minority, President Ramaphosa faces – like most of his peers on the African continent – the unavoidable challenge of unemployment, which officially stands at 34.5% of the total population, though it is far worse in the youth sector.[22]

Another dilemma is healthcare imbalance, including the controversial topic of universal health, rebranded in South Africa as National Health Insurance (NHI). Whatever the arguments between the private and the public sector, the reality is that South Africa has two healthcare systems. One is private, serving a minority of the population who can afford to pay increasingly exorbitant monthly as well as out-of-pocket fees. The other is public, funded mainly by tax revenues, and serving the vast majority of citizens. Although StatsSA found in 2017 that only 17 in 100 people have private medical insurance, the private sector healthcare spend (including medical schemes, out-of-pocket payments, medical insurance and employer private spend) was, at that time, 4.2% of GDP, versus 4.4% for the public sector (DPME, 2017). This unequal resourcing leads to unequal health outcomes that mirror the fault lines of race and geography inherited from apartheid.[23] This is, in all respects, a ticking social time bomb.

The challenge for any African leader, corporate or political, is to champion the adoption of new technology while responsibly transitioning its people to embrace it. Disruptive technology does just that – it disrupts, even if the socioeconomic impact is positive. A good example of finding this balance is Uber: a brilliant idea, but not without serious implications. Who would have imagined that lives would be tragically lost when traditional taxi operators, threatened by this "invasion" of their business model, attacked local Uber drivers, as has happened in South Africa.

It is also easy to see why there is great fear around artificial intelligence (AI) – but it represents a huge opportunity for Africa. In particular, it allows us to look at our challenges and see how we can use new technology platforms to turbocharge development and find our own solutions for continental growth and prosperity.

AI will become increasingly important for healthcare, education, food production and infrastructure development, and has the potential to catapult Africa into a bright new future. For instance, innovative research and applications in healthcare have the potential to encourage Africa to make significant progress in finding solutions to disease, such as malaria, HIV/Aids and now Covid-19. The message needs to be clear: AI is not the enemy!

Education will be radically transformed on the continent as new and more effective ways to inform and train the masses become ubiquitous. Agricultural production will also be transformed, and elevated to another level altogether, as African farmers use advanced technology for more productive crops and animal husbandry. The application of drones in the agricultural space is a case in point, as is the emergence and adoption of Controlled Environment Farming (CEF), including vertical greenhouse farming, and derelict-building conversions close to consumer communities.

The 2017 Global Innovation Index Report highlights that agriculture is leading innovation and development compared to all other areas of commerce and industry. This makes a lot of sense given the growing global population and rapidly increasing consumption of food – and surely there is no better source of food than the African continent. While the 2021 Global Innovation Index Report shows a significant shift, with pharmaceuticals now topping the table, this is not necessarily the result of lower demand for agricultural products worldwide, but rather because of the impact of Covid-19 and an increase in the demand for medicine.[24] Irrespective rankings, agriculture will continue to be a key target for innovation. Africa is fertile. It has vast areas of unused, fertile landmass, all within a healthy agricultural environment. It has the people. It has the will. And it is blessed with a good climate.

Agricultural capability is one of our "comparative advantages" as a continent, which is why I believe it would be sheer madness to industrialise at the expense of agriculture. A diversified economy is critical for development – but not at the expense of diluting our inherent ability to produce food.

Profile: From black America to African opportunity

I have always said that a true social capitalist in Africa is one who is able to identify African challenges and convert them into opportunities. Eugene Faison is one of that select group of people who has been able to do this – and do it remarkably well! As an African-

American, Eugene can trace his ancestry to the West African country of Benin, but he fell in love with Africa on a trip with his wife to Dakar, Senegal. Since then, as a businessman, he has invested incredible time and effort in understanding the territory.

I first bumped into Eugene about 10 years ago in a hotel in the bustling centre of Lusaka, Zambia. Our meeting was accidental. At the time I was on a tour of southern African countries, meeting clients and channel partners. Eugene was working with a young entrepreneurial incubator organisation in Zambia funded by USAID and some global corporates.

It is always refreshing to pick up the story of a descendant of Africa who has returned to his roots to contribute meaningfully. Birthed during the trans-Atlantic slave trade, African-American history is not without its own trauma, and there are still significant challenges affecting African-Americans in the US today. In order to understand Eugene's passion for the motherland, and to appreciate why we should encourage people like him to operate here, we need to understand something of his background.

Eugene was born in the late 1940s, a time when black people were still trying to make inroads into corporate America. His father was an entrepreneur, and from an early age Eugene was encouraged to "try things out", as he puts it – an approach that would hold him in good stead.

In 1984, Eugene became involved with the leadership of the Young Men's Christian Association (YMCA),[25] which was operating in emerging markets in Asia and Africa, providing economic solutions through a variety of programmes. In working with the YMCA leadership, he was able to start an NGO called the International Small Enterprise Development Centre (ISEDC), which provided technical assistance to productive small businesses. The US State Department provided Eugene with $1-million in start-up funding.

It was through this and subsequent initiatives that Eugene cut his teeth as a social capitalist in Africa. ISEDC facilitated SMEs in developing countries to get technical and sometimes financial guidance from experts, aligning the items they produced for the American market. For example, in Botswana some SMEs were making incredible baskets. To sell them in US floral markets, baskets needed 5-, 7- and 12-inch surfaces to cater for potted plants, in colours recommended by the Color Association of the United States. Another example was in Kenya, where

SMEs were making great leather wallets that did not fit the requirements and standards for US-issued credit cards.

By providing such technical insights, Eugene ended up successfully running this organisation and forming working relationships with heads of state and captains of industry. By the time I met him in Lusaka, he was leading an initiative in Zambia called YAPYA, which supported young entrepreneurs with technical skills and corporate funding. I was working for Sage, providing business management software for control and accountability in the incubated businesses.

Eugene and I developed a relationship, which saw us meet again more recently. I was then working for Deloitte and Eugene was driving Cold Chain Solutions in sub-Saharan Africa, using solar-powered components based on NASA technology. His products ensured that harvested vegetables in countries such as Kenya, which travel to market through high-temperature environments, maintain their freshness and quality. The same technology is also being used by hospitals in countries like Rwanda to ensure that medication being distributed in remote areas is conserved at the optimal temperature.

In all these initiatives, there is a priority to focus on the youth bulge that is affected by unemployment, wars, health epidemics, and so on. The success of these economic endeavours is measured not just by profit but by the power to build a self-sustaining capacity directed towards a brighter future.

Why did Eugene zoom in on Africa? He could easily have stayed comfortable in Washington DC and ignored the rest of the world. He could have focused on resolving his "back yard" problems. But he says he "got tired of seeing people taking all the resources and not giving back". And he wanted to "fish where the fish are".

With his gift for accessing a global network of investors interested in development in Africa, Eugene pours all his energy into this continent. He spends much of his time criss-crossing a vast economic landscape, driving business solutions that involve multinational corporations in the US while turning challenges into spectacular opportunities for the benefit of all. He is what I would call a "serial social-capitalist entrepreneur", and provides that exciting blend of capitalism and social solutions that Africa needs to lift it out of the doldrums.

In doing so, Eugene represents a group of people who are making things happen in Africa, who are not ashamed to make money – but who choose to do so with a social motive. People, in other words, who truly know how to Rumble in the Jungle.

Questions to ask yourself

- How well do you know the customer in the African market in which you want to do business?
- How well do you understand the landscape? For example, what are the legislative frameworks that could impact your business?
- Are you willing and able to provide an element of social-capitalism to your investment – one that is appropriate to the specific market you have targeted?

LESSON 2
INNOVATE

"A wise man never knows all,
only fools know everything."
Equatorial Guinea proverb

The fight: Rope-a-dope

Muhammad Ali was aware that, pound for pound, fist for fist, there was no way he could take out George Foreman, who was stronger and younger than he was. He also knew that doing the same thing while expecting a different result is madness. So one of the innovative techniques he used to tire Foreman was what came to be known as "rope-a-dope".

"Rope-a-dope" is a boxing technique where, instead of moving around the ring, the boxer chooses to lean back into the ropes for extended periods in order to avoid many of his opponent's heaviest blows.[1]

When the bell rang, he [Foreman] began to pound Ali with his signature sledgehammer blows, but the older man simply backed himself up against the ropes and used his arms to block as many hits as he could. He was confident that he could wait Foreman out.[2]

By thinking out of the box – in other words, being innovative – and applying a different, unexpected technique, Ali was able to beat a stronger opponent.

Round 2: Technology, the ultimate disruptor

Henry Mintzberg, a world-renowned academic and author on strategy, wrote a *Harvard Business Review*[3] paper in which he likened the formulation and implementation of strategy to a potter moulding clay. Mintzberg concluded that when a potter is moulding clay on the wheel, he has to be flexible – to the point that if the clay he is using is not up to standard, it is best to throw it away and start again with fresh clay.

Every ceramicist knows this. It is a fundamental of the trade, a foundation of the art.

The same principle can be applied in the African space. You have to have an adaptive, flexible strategy to successfully manoeuvre through the African terrain – which can be highly unpredictable at times. And sometimes, you need to start afresh.

In his book *Strategy Safari*, Mintzberg analyses a number of companies over a period of time and compares the original strategies that were formulated in the boardroom to the strategies that were eventually implemented to get the desired results. In the process, Mintzberg noticed a trend. When an organisation diverts from its strategic blueprint for one reason or another, they are adopting what he labelled "emergent strategies". The organisation still has the ultimate goal in mind, but allows flexibility in the implementation of its strategy. In this way, the organisation avoids "tunnel vision" and allows itself to adapt.

And adaptation has never been more necessary than in the rapidly changing technology space.

Having worked for one of the largest professional-services firms in the world, I get inundated with questions about digitisation, AI, augmented technology and virtual immersion. We are advancing swiftly into the digitally enabled world and the Fourth Industrial Revolution (see Figure 2.1), and people fear being sacrificed on the altar of efficiency and optimisation – which until recently seemed the stuff of science fiction.

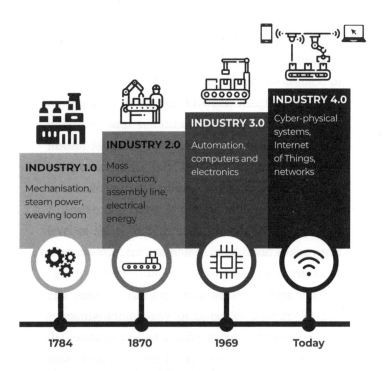

Figure 2.1 The Industrial Revolutions

In a sci-fi movie, it all goes wrong when the human race is obliterated by the takeover of machines, but from where I stand, the chances of it all going right for the human race are much more feasible. In reality, technology holds great promise for us as a species, and if history is anything to go by, our survival of the three previous Industrial Revolutions suggests we'll likely still be the main characters in the plot post-IR4.

Innovation is deeply embedded in the human genome. It stems back to our origins – an instinct built into our psyche and strengthened by an innate sense of survival. It is possibly the most powerful of our instincts; as humankind, we've been innovating for a long time. From man's earliest spears and tools, there has never been a time when innovation was absent from the human condition. And we continue to thrive (possibly too successfully) now that our defences and offensives in business are driven by technology.

It is imperative that we understand technology to be a friend, not a foe. There is great excitement in technology. Technology is releasing us from the grind of the mundane and inspiring our creative spirit to build a better world. We can do things, experience things and learn things we never could before.

The late Harvard author and lecturer on innovation, Clayton Christensen, wrote that, "Disruptive technologies typically enable new markets to emerge."[4] In other words, when we start thinking out of the box, new opportunities present themselves – and technology is inevitably the platform that facilitates this.

Technology helps technology. In these thrilling times, humankind is on a high: in an electrically charged atmosphere, technology is allowing innovative ideas to explode and grow exponentially. We have seen this with offerings like Uber and Airbnb – how these small start-ups have grown overnight, taking on large chunks of the traditional market. In December 2015, the *Harvard Business Review* showed how these disruptive start-ups initially capitalise the lower end of the market and then bulldoze their way into the big players' space, using the momentum of a new idea that makes sense and is embraced at volume by consumers. (See Figure 2.2, which is adapted from this article).)

Going back to the concerns and fears of Industry 4.0, what does this mean for Africa? Technological innovation will affect a developing economy more radically than a developed one, and the fact that Africa is predominantly an emerging market cannot be ignored. Governments, trade unions, youth and the general public are fearful in the face of the high unemployment levels evident throughout Africa. (The average youth unemployment on the continent is 10.6%, compared to a global average of 13.8% in 2021.[5] However, because of the mix of countries in Africa, this can vary significantly from country to country – for example, South Africa showed a figure of 20% in the same period.[6]) From an African perspective, I would rather risk being optimistic. Africa has always been great at leapfrogging and adopting new technologies early, and there are many examples of how technology can help (and is already helping) Africans.

Imagine how literacy levels could skyrocket by leveraging the existing, excellent telecoms infrastructure and new micro-learning techniques to educate children. The same applies to healthcare, which is already using telemedicine to provide people in remote areas with diagnoses and healthcare, saving them from having to travel long distances. Disease eradication is becoming more and more effective. Throughout Africa, drones are efficiently delivering medicines.

A digitised economy will significantly reduce

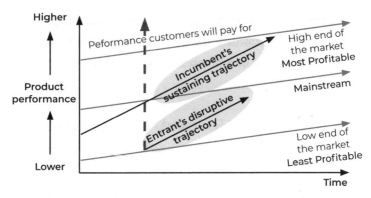

Figure 2.2 Innovation: Incumbents vs Disruptors [4]

the instability and uncertainty of printed money – something Africans are likely to energetically embrace, given the continent's regrettable history of graft and corruption. A cashless society may well have a better chance of rapid adoption in Africa than in other societies – and will in the process eliminate cash heists and needless loss of life. That noted, I am under no illusion about the inevitable rise of cybercrime. Industry 4.0 is no panacea for that particular problem.

Another positive impact of technology is seen in food production. With the global population growing and living longer, there will be increasing demand for both crops and livestock reared in a more efficient and sustainable manner. Figure 2.3 gives a taste of some of the innovative African agricultural and food industry technologies that are being developed to help meet the needs of a hungry world.[7]

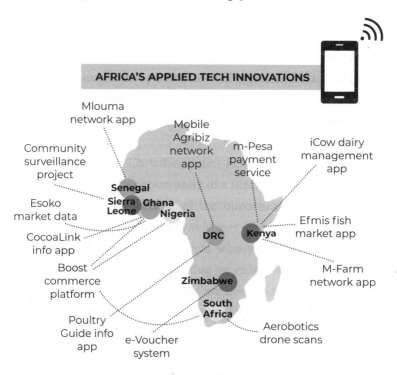

Figure 2.3 A sample of African innovations in the agri-tech space[7]

At the same time as Africa is driving towards industrialisation under 4IR, it faces the dilemma that its population will soon exceed 1.2 billion, the majority being young and employable. The more automated the continent becomes, the less hands-on labour is required. Africa is likely not big enough to digest the demand for employment that will arise (bearing in mind that, according to the IMF, Africa's GDP was less than 3% of global GDP in 2021). The only solution is to position our future workforce globally.

In Ghana, for example, cocoa farmers have been able to develop an app called CocoaLink (visible in the figure on p59), which allows them to share information on growing trends and market prices via their cellphones. This helps Ghana to be one of the leading cocoa suppliers in the world. Another innovation, in DRC, is an app called Poultry Guide, which has been developed using basic cellphone technology for farmers to share ideas on poultry, raising stock and mitigating for risks such as disease.

As these examples show, Africa is more than ready to benefit from 4IR. What it requires is that we become masters of these technologies. Whether solutions are home-grown or imported, success lies in identifying an opportunity or problem, and then using technology to find a solution. Africans are used to finding solutions with little or nothing to go on – so it is no surprise that a significant number of technological solutions developed in Africa are now being exported globally (in addition to the ever-popular M-Pesa). Hopefully the owners of these technologies have sought protection to ensure that the royalties and profits from their IP are repatriated to continue developing the continent and its people.

"Float like a butterfly, sting like a bee."
Muhammad Ali

Round 3: Unlocking African-ness

Africa encourages co-creation. A mutually supportive ecosystem is the very essence of life in Africa – and it's a far cry from the traditional silo structures of Western business. Is it possible that this is the way of the business future?

Africa needs to develop innovative thinkers and "actioners", people who are able to Rumble in the Jungle by bringing together tangible capital (traditional assets like money, technology and property) and intangible capital (relationships and networks) to fuel business in Africa's unique ecosystem. In his book *Nuts & Bolts*, McLean Sibanda makes an interesting argument for moving away from aid and instead promoting innovation and entrepreneurship.[8]

When it comes to technology, as a continent, Africa is in a conundrum. Where we are now is not where we were 100 years ago, and is not where we'll be even 10 years from now. We need a generation of businesspeople who are able to look at Africa not as an isolated continent but as an integral part of the global mix, a player able to provide transversal solutions that cut across political, environmental, social, technological, legal and economic (PESTLE) lines. We need solutions that are "glocal", in other words – global solutions with local relevance. Individuals such as Sajeed Sacranie, who we will meet later, exemplify this awareness, not just for older generations but also for the next generation of leaders.

It is mind-blowing to think that five of the biggest companies in the world – Facebook, Amazon, Apple, Netflix and Google (Alphabet) (the FAANGs) – could be valued at considerably more than US$5-

trillion (as of writing), while Africa's entire GDP is estimated to be around US$2.5-trillion. That Africa's 54 countries produce less than half of these five companies' net worth is a scary reality. Nevertheless, if you track the average year-on-year growth of these companies, you will note that Africa is providing some of the highest growth rates in the world, due to the penetrative opportunities that exist here.

I host many talks about doing business in Africa, in which one of the key topics is innovation and how vital it is for Africa to innovate, not only for its own benefit but for global export. Such was my determination to promote this idea that I began work on a keynote address entitled "African Intelligence". It was only after drafting a few paragraphs that I realised the abbreviation for my new keynote is "AI".

Artificial intelligence.

Why is Africa not at the forefront of producing innovative ideas? If "necessity is the mother of invention", our calabash should be overflowing with innovations. Are we coming up with innovative ideas but not scaling them? Are these ideas dying a premature death? Or perhaps we don't market our ideas adequately, so that people who invest don't know about them? Whichever it is, something radical must be done to fill this vacuum so the continent can achieve its potential.

Personal experience: Staying flexible in Nigeria

In 2010, I was working at Sage Plc, a business-management software company listed on the London Stock Exchange (LSE) as well as on the FTSE 100. The regional office was based in Johannesburg, South Africa, but our territory included sub-Saharan Africa, the Middle East and Australasia. Gartner, a leading technology-research company, rated my employer in the top three companies in the global market, which included Oracle and SAP.

As a global player, we had just over three million customers, with an annual turnover of £1.3-billion. The company was tried and tested, and had been in existence for close to 30 years. It was growing at an average rate of 6% per annum. This background is key, because it explains why we (at that time unknowingly) positioned ourselves as George Foreman in the African-market "boxing ring".

As a member of the executive, which was primarily responsible for growing our markets in the African region, I was tasked with leading the team responsible for increasing our share of the Nigerian market. Back then, Nigeria had a population of about 159 million and a GDP approaching US$365-billion.[9] Research suggested that the Nigerian market was poised for growth – not just because of the population size, but also because of the level of foreign direct investment that was going into the country.

We believed that the software solution we had so successfully introduced to small start-up businesses, and which was leading the market in southern Africa, would be appropriate to help us grow the Nigerian market. Based on this market feedback, and with the support of our global brand, we believed we had the winning ticket. Our thinking was to rapidly gain market share by discounting our retail launch price by 70% per CD, from US$100 to US$30, thus creating volumes to underpin margin recovery going forward. The formula was simple: by creating volumes, we'd ensure recovery and surplus in the long term through annuity income-related services.

After numerous flights between Johannesburg and Lagos, significant investment through marketing (which included events and expensive campaign adverts), as well as multiple meetings with our Nigerian channel partners, who would have thought it would deliver zilch? The return on investment (ROI) for all our hard work was... almost zero.

As the person responsible for leading the initiative, I was deeply concerned. I believed that our product was good and our strategy correct, as demonstrated by the success we'd achieved with the same model in South Africa, Africa's biggest economy, as well as more mature economies such as the US and certain countries in Europe.

Our failure in the Nigerian market did not make sense.

With its "small start-up" entrepreneurial culture, Nigeria should have been completely receptive to our offering. Even if just 1% of a population of 159 million invested in our solution, that would equate to 1.6 million start-ups – a significant market. That would be a jackpot compared to South Africa, where the number of businesses in the same space, using our product, did not even get to 300,000!

In hindsight, our aggressive approach to grow the Nigerian market as fast as possible by heavily discounting the retail price of our product had unwelcome consequences.

It was on one of my trips to Lagos (which, I may add, were becoming increasingly depressing because of the dilemma we were facing), that I had my eureka moment. This was thanks to a colleague based in Nigeria, who was more familiar with the local market than I was. He pointed out that our strategy was bound to fail in the Nigerian context – and he took me to a suburb in Lagos called Ikeja, near the international airport. Here we entered an informal market, ironically named Computer Village.

It was an encounter I will never forget. The market was about the size of a football stadium, with all kinds of electronic wares being hawked, from cellphones to computer software and hardware. Having had politely asked me to reserve my comments until later, my host led me through the throng of people crowding the marketplace to a vendor who had a suitcase packed with CDs.

To my surprise, my host asked the vendor for the exact software we were selling in the Nigerian market. Without hesitation, the vendor dipped into his suitcase of CDs and extracted what looked like a close imitation of our original software CD – although the branding on the CD cover bore a painfully poor resemblance to the legal original. My host then asked the vendor for the price. To my shock and horror, the vendor replied that the going price was US$1 – but that it was negotiable!

Bear in mind that after heavily discounting the product (by 70%), we were retailing the same item at US$30. I was speechless. I had always known that piracy in the Nigerian market was pervasive – but experiencing it first-hand was something I was unprepared for.

Recognising the challenge, I went on to research Computer Village to help me understand the extent of the threat to our legal trading, and was overwhelmed by the extent of informal, illegal trading and counterfeiting. The most sobering statistic was that Computer Village's estimated annual turnover was a whopping US$2-billion – 54% more than a company listed on the LSE that had been around for close to 30 years and had three million clients in 52 countries!

We knew that trying to fight the piracy stronghold in Nigeria would be futile. The only way was to change our strategy and focus our efforts on marketing our enterprise suite of products, to medium and large MNCs directly – since MNCs were required by global mandate to invest in legal software. This change in approach did not give us the level of penetration we would have liked in our start-up phase – but our year-on-year revenue growth was spectacular, with some of our product lines growing by more than 100% year on year.

As Einstein said, "Insanity is doing the same thing over and over again and expecting different results."

Computer Village

Nigerian Guy Narrates How He Paid N8000 (US$20) For Nokia Phone Filled With Fufu (dough) At Computer Village, Ikeja

– Blog entry

Case study 2.1: Thinking out of the box in Rwanda

At a function a few years ago, I was having a discussion with a colleague from Rwanda. He asked me what I thought of the Rwandan government's decision to sign a "sleeve-sponsoring deal" with Premier League club Arsenal. This involves an advert that simply says "Visit Rwanda" placed in a 20-square-centimetre ad-patch on players' jersey sleeves, and running for a period of three years.

The cost? A cool US$39-million.

At first glance this seems a little crazy. But here's the Rwandan government's rationale: in 2017, tourists visiting Rwanda contributed 12.7% to GDP, equating to about US$400-million in revenue. The government sees upmarket leisure tourism and convention tourism as an important growth sector, and Rwanda has a lot going for it as a destination: lush green landscapes, the mountain gorillas of the Virunga volcanoes, the Akagera National Park, the tropical Nyungwe forest, the idyllic Lake Kivu, and even its genocide memorials – all compressed into a space of just 26,000 square kilometres.

By 2019, the contribution of tourism to the GDP had grown to 15%, at a value of US$1.6-billion.[10]

In its Economic Development and Poverty Reduction Strategy II, 2013-2018 (EDPRS II), Rwanda states an ambition to raise GDP per capita to US$1,000; reduce the percentage of the population living below the poverty line to less than 30%; and reduce the percentage of the population living in extreme poverty to less than 9%. These goals were built on development successes over the last decade that included high growth, rapid poverty reduction and reduced inequality. Between 2001 and 2021, real GDP growth went from 8.48% to 10.88% per annum.[11] Based on this, one can say that Rwanda's president Paul Kagame is doing something right.

Initially, I was sceptical about Rwanda's sleeve promotion, regardless of how it was rationalised. My gut instinct, supported by my traditional values, was against the whole idea. I thought, *Here's another African government wasting taxpayers' valuable money...*

But biased though I am (being a staunch Chelsea fan!) I changed my mind.

Rwanda has been a pioneer of socio-economic reform on the continent, spurring a number of other African countries to follow its example. Perhaps the sleeve-ads were a stroke of sheer genius, considering that more than a million people watch each Arsenal game live on television. If you extrapolate that over three years, that's a huge amount of publicity in anyone's book.

Who would ever have thought, given Rwanda's experience of one of the worst genocides in recent history, in 1994, that the country would start selling itself on the world stage in such a manner?

As Africans, we have historically been burdened with the stigma of living on the "dark continent".

Millions of people seeing the Rwandan brand being broadcast on international television would be, to me at least, a big achievement. Their only challenge would be to follow through on such a large national investment – there would be nothing more disappointing than a country marketing itself so aggressively, and then not delivering results.

More recently, it was announced that Rwanda had worked in partnership with NBA Africa to build a basketball auditorium to host the inaugural Basketball Africa League[12] tournament in the first half of 2020. Unfortunately the start date had to be delayed because of Covid-19, but the inaugural season eventually began in May 2021. The Basketball Africa League is evidence of the exciting ideas that are emerging as a result of the commitment of the country's leadership and a global sports multinational company like the NBA.

Case study 2.2: Achieving the extraordinary in Senegal

Another big story is the fact that Senegal won the rights to host the fourth edition of the summer Youth Olympic Games 2022 (YOG) in the capital, Dakar –

an event that has been postponed to 2026 due to the Covid-19 pandemic.

Senegal is a small West African country with a population of just over 17 million and a GDP of US$25-billion – tiny when compared to Africa's economic giants, such as South Africa (GDP US$420-billion) and Nigeria (GDP US$441-billion). Dakar is already well known as a vibrant city, famous for its lively markets and rich musical culture. It also boasts beautiful colonial architecture, secluded beaches blessed with world-famous surf breaks, and remote riverine deltas teeming with wildlife.

Senegal is also one of the countries in Africa that has a Junior NBA Academy, which certainly would have helped with their Olympic bid. The current NBA vice-president and managing director for Africa, Amadou Gallo Fall, is of Senegalese origin, and has played a key role in driving the growth of this sport on the African continent, especially among the younger generation. Senegal has had its share of other sporting heroes – notably Sadio Mane, an international soccer player who has played for Liverpool.

I know there are sceptics who question the wisdom of hosting expensive ventures like the Olympics. I have also noted our tendency in Africa to engage in convoluted argument, often to the point where it's counterproductive; in trying to resolve some problems, we end up throwing out the baby with the bathwater. Either way, I will always remember the look on my son's face when I took him to one of the 2010 Football World Cup games (Brazil vs Ivory Coast) in South Africa. He was in awe – and that is the reward for imagining an Africa that's alive with possibility.

Senegal created a spotlight for itself, highlighted its positive attributes and is now nurturing the dreams of a new generation of local boys and girls who will be able to contribute to and participate in the Youth Olympics. For that, I will stand and applaud.

Case study 2.3: The most innovative company in Africa

Zipline, a San Francisco-based company focused on Africa, was highlighted by *Fast Company*, a leading US business magazine, as the 10th most-innovative company in the world, and top in Africa. In this ranking, Snap (parent company to Snapchat) was number one in the world, followed by Microsoft and Tesla. Launched in 2016 in Kigali, Rwanda, Zipline uses drone technology to transport blood supplies to remote parts of Rwanda. It is now responsible for 75% of the blood distribution in Kigali,[13] quite an accomplishment. In May 2019, Zipline moved into Ghana – and in less than a year reached 2,000 hospitals, catering to 12 million people.

I get excited by successful stories such as Zipline's for a number of reasons. First, those familiar with the African landscape will know of the lack of transport and cold-chain infrastructure in rural areas, which makes it difficult to transport blood for emergency transfusions. Using drones to overcome this challenge once again shows how problems can be resolved with an innovative solution.

Second, the company that owns Zipline is based in the US, in Silicon Valley, the hub of global technology innovation – yet it is providing a profitable solution for its shareholders through an African offering. This is also a key point: for Africa to be successful in resolving its problems, it will need to tap into global IP solutions.

Last but not least, the Zipline story resonates with my strong belief that to identify the opportunities in Africa, you need first to identify a problem.

As highlighted by the company's CEO and co-founder Keller Rinaudo, the story of Zipline is a stand-out example of a multinational being successful in Africa. Zipline learnt how to work with Rwanda's civil aviation regulator, integrate with the public healthcare supply chain, set up distribution centres, and manage the maintenance of the drones in the country.

Profile: Innovation, Ubuntu-style

Sajeed Sacranie had a brilliant, innovative mind. I had the pleasure of working with him over the years, and he became one of my mentors, helping me gain perspective when business in Africa was not quite business as usual. What strengthened our relationship was our shared vision of Africa – a continent with a wealth of opportunity. Sadly, in 2021, Sajeed passed away from Covid-19 complications. I will miss our coffee chats, but will always remember the inspiration we shared on how to make Africa a better place.

I first met Sajeed when I was working at Deloitte South Africa, carrying the portfolio of business development for my division. Our team's primary role was to work with the rest of the leadership in identifying and harnessing opportunities that would lead to revenue growth.

Selling professional services is a tough gig, especially for me, having come from selling software that was very much commoditised. At the time, Sajeed was a strategic adviser to the executive leadership of Deloitte. To be a trusted adviser to the leadership of a global audit and advisory firm, you have to have the credentials, backed (more importantly) by industry experience. Every time I sat with him to discuss our business-development strategy, I could not help but feel awe at how he could rethink situations with his unique combination of experience and enthusiasm.

Sajeed was born in Malawi, into an Indian family that had settled in Africa in the late 1800s. He identified himself as cosmopolitan: Indian by origin, African by birth, with a colonial education. He got his first taste of the unpredictable corporate world when he landed a job with Barings – a prestigious merchant bank at the time, with a 300-year history that included being Queen Elizabeth's banker.

In 1995, a cataclysmic event occurred in his life that made him reflect on his purpose and destiny. He was sitting in his office in corporate London when the CFO advised him that £100-million had disappeared from one of their client's accounts. This turned out to be part of the events initiated by the infamous Nick Leeson, a Barings Bank trader in the Singapore office who had passed through a number of fraudulent transactions that caused the bank to make losses of more than £200-million – at the time, almost half of the bank's capital.[14]

This bankruptcy delivered a number of life lessons for Sajeed, and triggered his passion for innovative thinking and making an impact in the start-up and venture-capital world. His drive was spotted by Richard Branson, who handpicked Sajeed to launch Virgin Mobile in South Africa. After completing the assignment, Sajeed became an independent adviser, giving valuable input on innovative thinking to a number of corporates in Africa, including Deloitte. Another person he impressed was the legendary South African businessman Kaizer Motaung, who took him on as an adviser for Kaizer Chiefs – probably the biggest and wealthiest football club in Africa, with close to 14 million supporters; a very grassroots, predominantly black, soccer club.

This ability to straddle the highest levels of Western capitalism and deeply African business is a rare skill. Sajeed branded himself as a rainmaker whose identity as an African broke boundaries. He developed his own niche in advising multinationals by taking their discussions from the boardroom to around the fireplace. He had another powerful skill: as a man in his mid-50s, he could easily sit in a room with Millennials and impress them. He believed that, sometimes, the solutions to Africa's problems were simple and were staring us in the face.

"Ubuntu" is a South African word which, translated, means "I am, because we are", or "in order to be successful, we need to work together". One of the key lessons I learnt from Sajeed is that Ubuntu is not just a social concept; it should be used to transform the way in which Africa does business with the rest of the world. "Cut and paste" Western models do not work here; to be successful in Africa, you need relevant but innovative solutions.

Questions to ask yourself

- Is your company being innovative enough in its African strategy?
- What is it that you have to *unlearn* in order to be innovative?
- Can you solve a specifically African problem with the use of technology?

KNOW YOUR THREATS

"A fly that dances carelessly
in front of a spider's web risks
the wrath of the spider's teeth."
Ivorian proverb

The fight: Big mouth

In one of the many pre-fight press conferences, Muhammad Ali had parodied George Foreman: the reigning champion had a reputation for stalking his opponents, moving as mechanically as Frankenstein's monster in his pursuit of victory. By the third round, Ali's joke didn't seem so funny.

George Foreman [was] a giant of a man, a fearsome specimen of gleaming muscle with the cold, dead eyes of someone who has seen much more of the human condition than society deems healthy... Without mercy or the slightest sign of empathy, Foreman pursued the former champion around the 20-foot ring, launching punches from odd angles, swinging hooks and power shots that thudded into Ali's body, inhuman blows that seemed too much for any man to withstand.[1]

As much as Ali had a big mouth, he had gauged and prepared for the very real threat of George Foreman. He had studied Foreman's tactics and never underestimated his brutal strength. The threat was significant, but Ali had already called it. He knew exactly what he was facing.

In *The Art of War*, the great general of China, Sun Tzu, wrote, "If you know the enemy and know yourself, you need not fear the result of a hundred battles." The same applies when doing business in Africa: the only way to navigate around the threats and challenges – and ultimately survive them – is to accurately identify them first.

Round 4: Forewarned is forearmed

There is a saying that when America sneezes, the rest of the world catches a cold. In other words: when things go wrong with the world's leading economy, it affects economies across the globe. This was evident with the financial crisis of 2008, which was triggered globally by the reckless financing of the US housing market by major banks such as Bear Stearns and Lehman Brothers.

Over the years, the rest of world has had to brace itself in one way or another in dealing with threats from the US or Europe – so much so that nobody anticipated *China* catching a cold, literally. Having originated supposedly in China, the threat of Covid-19's global pandemic came out of left field and rattled all the PESTLE (political, economic, social, technological, legal and environmental) frameworks that had given us a certain level of comfort – false comfort, as it transpired.

With its inadequate healthcare systems, Africa was in danger of facing a threat of massive proportions. The crisis might have become catastrophic had it not been for the bold, proactive measures taken by presidents Nana Akufo-Addo (Ghana), Paul Kagame (Rwanda) and Cyril Ramaphosa (South Africa), all of whom imposed temporary economic and social lockdowns. Even the much-needed African Continental Free Trade Area (AfCFTA), which was due to be launched in July 2020 and expected to unlock close to US$3-trillion, was postponed until January 2021.

Nothing is certain, as they say, except death and taxes. You can plan for some threats, as Ali did in the ring, but others demand that you think on your feet – and Ali did a fair amount of that too. In both cases, the sooner you are able to identify the threat, the sooner you are able to respond – and succeed.

Round 5: Take nothing for granted

What is the greatest threat to doing business in Africa? One school of thought would say it is lack of access to financing; another would say it is the high country-to-continent density, which means that navigating through each country leads to having to figure out new market-entry barriers. Others say it's the corruption, weak governance systems and instability caused by wars. I recall my managing director telling me about a conversation he'd had with a colleague from an emerging market country not in Africa. After noting the economic ramifications of poor leadership in a particular African country, this colleague had said that "Africa never missed the opportunity to miss an opportunity".

Being an African realist, I was initially offended by this. How dare they be so dismissive of the challenges we face! But it did get me thinking about how many times we have done ourselves no favours by making bad decisions or impeding our own success. While I am fully aware that those in First World countries make similar mistakes, the difference is they have the luxury of stronger economies that are able to bounce back. After the storming of the US Capitol in 2021, or the difficulties of implementing Brexit, both the US and Europe are still on relatively healthy growth trajectories. By contrast, Africa, whose GDP is less than 3% of the global GDP, battles to recover when anything similar happens here.

Does this mean there is no hope for us?

No – but it does mean we have a steeper hill to climb, and we can't afford unnecessary slip-ups. And knowing the threats to development in Africa is fundamental for any business or organisation wanting to remain competitive and achieve dominance in the African landscape.

Business threats are those factors that come from the external environment and over which the organisation has no control. Often these threats come from the traditional PESTLE factors, which these days can be exacerbated by the rapid rise of technological automation.

Fortunately, there are two primary interrelated actions that can be taken to counter these threats. The first is to identify the threat and understand it for what it is. Second, it is vital to act on the threat to mitigate the consequences for you and/or your organisation.

Muhammad Ali was a big talker, but he still knew that George Foreman was a dangerous opponent. Physically and psychologically, he had to prepare himself to face his opponent – and plan how to beat him. Any successful sportsman will tell you that half the battle is won in your head. By understanding the threat you face, you can develop a strategy to win.

In my PhD research,[2] I investigated MNCs operating on the African continent. I surveyed 125 C-level executives from a cross-section of industries in South Africa, Kenya, Nigeria and Egypt. The primary objective of my research was to determine the key institutional factors and/or external factors that contributed to the success (or failure) of the business. From the research, two environmental factors were most often identified by executives.

The first was the stability of the judiciary; in particular, its independence from the political leadership. An example may be found in the respective conditions of South Africa and Zimbabwe. In South Africa, the independence of the judiciary allows for current and former presidents to be put on trial when warranted, as we saw in the case of former president Jacob Zuma, who is (albeit years later) awaiting trial on multiple corruption charges. In Zimbabwe, the judiciary was significantly compromised during Robert Mugabe's rule. The impact of the judiciary's independence (or lack thereof) on these countries' economic stability is clear.

The second factor is that of national security: the level of safety and security provided to a country's citizens. War, for example – in addition to the great cost of extreme human suffering and the decimation of a nation – can have a devastating impact on an economy, killing any prospect of growth. To use the example of South Africa and Zimbabwe again: while both countries are at peace, South Africa has to contend with the challenge of a high crime rate, which warrants concern for would-be investors. Zimbabwe, as a result of over a decade of farm invasions, is going through a prolonged economic meltdown, with dire consequences for its citizens.

While such conditions remain well beyond the control of MNCs, factors such as these need to be considered and analysed in terms of their potential threat to business. As with Ali, success comes from strategically navigating through them.

> *"No-one knows what to say in the loser's locker room."*
> **Muhammad Ali**

Personal experience: A lesson in leadership

There is a day so deeply ingrained in my memory that it seems like yesterday. I was a teenager in my last year of high school, an all-boys Catholic mission school in the province of Mashonaland, Zimbabwe. We had invited a patron, an alumnus of the school, to a fundraising event, and for this special day we were dressed in our Sunday best, shirts ironed and shoes polished. The day before our VIP guest arrived, his advance security team had already established themselves on the property – even on the rooftops of the school buildings. Hours before his appearance, we perched on every vantage point we could find, our excitement and fascination with the guards and their rifles palpable.

And then the moment arrived. With great fanfare, the motorcade drove in, sirens blaring, surrounded by yet more guards and yet more rifles. As the dust settled, there was our patron: none other than the then-president of the Republic of Zimbabwe, Robert Gabriel Mugabe. As we sat on the ground, Mugabe strode past us in his usual elegant style, as if looking down on us lesser mortals. I was one of the students in the first row, and I remember exchanging a glance with the great leader – I vividly recall the excitement, fear and elation I felt in that moment. To me at that time, legends like Nelson Mandela and Kwame Nkrumah paled in comparison to the great liberation hero at whose feet I was sitting. I had nothing but admiration for the articulate statesman, a former student of my very school. As a teenager with ambitions, I was in awe.

Fast-forward two decades.

At the age of 96, Mugabe was unceremoniously dethroned after leading a disastrous land-reform programme that precipitated Zimbabwe's rapid economic decline with unparalleled hyperinflation and a mass exodus of its people. The president had knowingly led his country into economic and political isolation. Lives were lost as the main opposition, the MDC, led by the late Morgan Tsvangirai, dared turn against him. Many companies, both local and foreign, were unprepared for this threat that devastated the once-powerful southern African economy.

Looking at the catastrophe that hit Zimbabwe, it is deeply painful to reflect on the leader I had so admired. How did this happen? Was it all just plunder and power-mongering at the expense of the Zimbabwean people? Was it pure arrogance and greed?

Today, not much has changed. There is a new man in charge, one who also rules with an iron fist. I could never have imagined the atrocities I would witness in my beloved homeland. Is this the best we can do in a once-wealthy and peaceful country? Did we learn nothing from the Rhodesian conflict? Are we doomed to self-destruct?

When I look around the world, my suspicion grows that the quality of leadership is the culprit. It is an antiquated and toxic leadership based on military dogma that has created Zimbabwe's low-intensity civil war. And my people deserve so much better.

Round 6: The threat of the leadership gap

The Oxford Dictionary defines leadership as the act of leading a group of people or an organisation. Looking at leadership in Africa, does the "wrong leadership" really just suggest that the science of leadership *itself* is wrong?

The World Economic Forum's global leadership index report for 2015 rated the level of public confidence of citizens in the respondent countries.[3] The Index used 37 indicators to effectively capture the perceptions of and challenges facing global leadership. The final results ranked leadership across national and regional boundaries, as well as by sector. On a scale of 1 to 10, with 1 being the worst perception of leadership and 10 being the best, Africa had a score of 4.3, which was not too bad compared to the global average of 4.25. Europe had the highest score of 4.54 and North America – surprisingly – the lowest score at 3.93.

Significantly, these figures highlight that while Africa does have challenges when it comes to leadership, we are little different from the rest of the world. In fact, based on this information, we rate highly enough to be able to give North America and Australia some tips![4]

But, as with my story about Robert Mugabe, we do experience particular challenges in Africa. One of these is that we cling to our struggle heroes to give us hope and guidance for a more cohesive society in the future.

The late Christian author Leonard Ravenhill once wrote, "The opportunity of a lifetime must be seized within the lifetime of the opportunity." We could also consider that it was Moses who led the Israelites out of Egypt, but Joshua who took them into the Promised Land. Looking at examples like that of Mugabe, it is likely that we need a different type of leadership to address the new dispensation.

Thanks to our forefathers, the liberation war heroes of their time – the likes of Jomo Kenyatta, Julius Nyerere, Kwame Nkrumah, Robert Mugabe, Samora Machel, Patrice Lumumba, Gamal Abdel Nasser and, of course, Nelson Mandela – Africa is politically free today. Their leadership took Africa out of the bondage of colonialism and apartheid to the promise of freedom – and they should be celebrated for that.

It reminds me of the story about US civil rights activist Martin Luther King Jr, who was assassinated in 1968. After his death, his widow, Cora, was asked by a journalist, "Is it not a shame that he never got to see the freedom he dreamt of?" Cora responded, "It is precisely because of his vision for a new era of freedom that we are here today."

The future leaders in Africa are facing different challenges to their forebears – and it is likely that a new generation of leaders, with different strengths, is needed to take Africa into the future. In the same way that Moses handed the baton to Joshua, the great liberation leaders should pass on leadership to the next generation in their recently liberated countries.

Significantly, future African leaders will have to tackle the challenge of poverty. Graph 3.1 over the page indicates that a significant percentage of the African population survives on less than US$1.90 per day. Graph 3.2 suggests that a more inclusive economy – one aligned with global standards – would help to even out the playing field.

KNOW YOUR THREATS

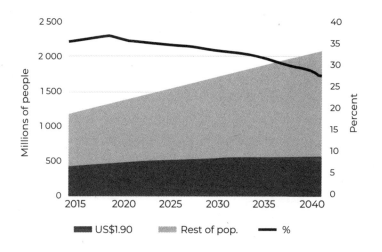

Graph 3.1 On Current Path: Africa Population and Extreme Poverty @ US$1.90

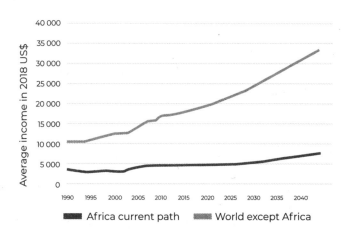

Graph 3.2 Average income per person 1980 to 2040 (PPP)

When we go to the polls to elect our heads of state, it's a shame that, as Africans, we are often inclined to assess leadership in terms of wealth, fame or liberation legacy while ignoring truer qualities of leadership. There are exceptions, however. Here are six leaders from different corners of the continent whose conduct reflects the essential qualities of leadership.

Mo Ibrahim

After making a fortune in the telecommunications industry, this Sudanese-British businessman paid it forward by creating an incentive to reward presidents for great leadership through the Mo Ibrahim Foundation, established in 2006.

Strive Masiyiwa

True to his name, entrepreneur Strive Masiyiwa fought an uphill battle to obtain a telecommunications licence in Zimbabwe, and went on to lead a trans-African organisation called Econet Holdings from modest beginnings. (For more on his story, see Lesson 5.)

Ellen Johnson Sirleaf

The 24th president of Liberia, Ellen Johnson Sirleaf was Africa's first elected female head of state. Having assumed her presidency in 2006, she was re-elected in 2011. She is known for her rigorous, non-violent fight for women's rights and safety, for which she was awarded the Nobel Peace Prize in 2011. In 2013, she was awarded the Indira Gandhi Prize. In 2014 and 2015, Sirleaf ranked 70th and 96th respectively on the *Forbes* list of most powerful women in the world.

Her leadership shows what heights a woman of valour can reach on the African stage. She once said, "If your dreams do not scare you, then they are not big enough." She has proven to be a robust leader, even in the face of a deadly Ebola outbreak that occurred in Liberia.

Abdel Fattah el-Sisi

Abdel Fattah Saeed Hussein Khalil el-Sisi is the sixth president of Egypt, and has been in office since 2014. He continues to fight against the terrorism that threatens the entire Arab region, and succeeded in averting civil war in Egypt after the ousting of president Mohamed Morsi. Sisi is pursuing much-needed economic reforms in Egypt and is seen by the West as a moderate force in the region. He was named one of the world's most outstanding leaders in the *Forbes* 2014 international rating.

Kofi Annan

The late Kofi Annan was originally a Ghanaian diplomat. In 2001, Annan and the United Nations were the co-recipients of the Nobel Peace Prize for their work in promoting peace and prosperity, and Annan's impressive CV of achievements led to his serving as the seventh secretary-general of the United Nations from January 1997 to December 2006.

After the terrorist attacks in the US in September 2001, Annan played a crucial role in encouraging the General Assembly and the Security Council to take action in combating terrorism. He faced a strong backlash for his delay in responding to the Rwandan genocide, but will nevertheless be remembered for the impact he made as the first African at the helm of the United Nations.

Ngozi Okonjo-Iweala

Ngozi Okonjo-Iweala is an internationally recognised Nigerian economist, best known for her two terms as finance minister of Nigeria and for her work at the World Bank, including as managing director from 2007 to 2011.

Okonjo-Iweala was the architect of policies that enabled Nigeria, today Africa's largest economy, to grow at an average of 6% per annum over three years. She is credited with developing reform programmes that improved governmental transparency and stabilised the economy. She was named by *Forbes* as the 44th and 48th most powerful woman in the world in the years 2014 and 2015.

Two other leaders in particular excite me today, not because they are perfect, but because they have taken over troubled countries and immediately implemented remedial actions. Their actions suggest that we are in for a great ride!

The first is the prime minister of Ethiopia, Abiy Ahmed, who in 2018 took over the leadership of the country at the relatively young age of 40. He immediately began to make amends with Eritrea, Ethiopia's neighbour, thus calming an antagonistic relationship spanning many years. Another thing he did was appoint a cabinet containing a large contingent of women – including the first female chief justice in the country's history. Ethiopia has gone through significant challenges in recent years, which have tested Ahmed's leadership as well as his credibility. Depending on who you talk to, the "jury is still out" on his handling of the latest crisis. The point remains that being a leader in Africa – whether young or old – is never a bed of roses.

The second is João Lourenço, the president of Angola, who in 2017 ended the decades-long stranglehold of José Eduardo dos Santos and his family. Lourenço immediately made bold and unheard-of decisions on existing corruption and leadership failings.

These positive developments highlight the emergence of a new generation of leaders and the comforting prospect of leaders who are trying to raise the bar in Africa, putting their countries on a path of rapid development after years of stagnation.

Enlightened African leaders understand that Africa is uniquely placed to feed a growing global population. Meeting this challenge will take Africa to a completely new level, opening the door for an African renaissance. Africa's new breed of leaders is eminently capable of achieving this to catapult the continent into a great future. And for those looking to invest in Africa, it is well worth identifying which leaders are of this new breed, and which are of old stock – and to act accordingly.

Case study 3.1: Sabotage in Angola

It was 2006, and the company I was working for had won a significant deal to supply an "accounting and retail software solution" to one of the largest distributors of Unilever products in Angola. This distributor had a presence not only in Angola, but in the rest of Africa too. The incentive was huge: if we were successful in rolling out the retail solution in Angola, the client would open up other African countries to us. Running into millions of US dollars, it was one of those mouthwatering deals that comes once in a lifetime.

To illustrate further how lucrative this marriage was: in 2006, Angola had a GDP of US$42-billion[5] and a population of 20 million people.[6] A leading exporter of crude oil in Africa, according to a KPMG report[7], Angola had surged ahead, developing the biggest fast-moving consumer goods (FMCG) industry in Africa. The report estimated that between 2000 and 2013 the market was to grow by a compound annual growth rate (CAGR) of at least 35% – with the nearest rival, Nigeria, having a CAGR of only 25%. So here we had secured a client that was one of the global leaders in the FMCG space, was operating in a market targeted to grow exponentially in the next 10 years, and had committed to partner with us into the rest of the continent.

What could possibly go wrong?

Well, first, we had severely underestimated the social aspect. Angola, a former Portuguese colony, is a Lusophone country, with Portuguese the main language of communication. As the service provider, our South African team in Angola spoke only English. And while we did have a Portuguese "channel partner" who assisted with translation, that was easier said than done. Another complexity was that the owners of the company were shrewd Lebanese businessmen who favoured the idea of importing labour from India to reduce costs. The cultural and language concoction that resulted was untenable.

There was a lot of money at stake, and Angola at the time ranked in the top 30 most corrupt countries in the world as listed by the Corruption Perceptions Index.[8] The project was already at risk of failure due to communication issues, and this only aggravated the situation.

From day one, we encountered endless challenges. But given the long-term value of the project, our attitude was to suffer now and reap the rewards later. We'd undertaken a number of similar projects remotely from South Africa, so why would we not succeed on this one? Even when we began to make a loss on the project, we persevered.

While communication with the client and their staff appeared to be the biggest problem, as it turned out, it was not the only one. We could never have foreseen a deliberate and focused attempt to sabotage the project. Things went from bad to worse: the owners of the business pretended to be unable to decipher some of their problems, but then used us as their scapegoat. It got to a point where we had to cut our losses and extract ourselves from the project.

Some time afterwards, we found out "unofficially" that, because of the significant amount of money involved, the project was doomed from the start – driven by an internal conspiracy involving clandestine client staff sabotage. This was confirmed by other vendors we came to know, who pointed out that one had regularly to meet challenges like these in Angola. The only practical way of mitigating the risk was by having a strong but reliable local business partner, who would be able to overcome the impediments to foreign firms. Soon after ending our project, our company as we knew it ceased to exist.

The specific lesson here was that, in certain instances, a local business partner may be a necessary cost of doing business. The greater lesson is that every market in Africa is different – and understanding the nature of the threats is key to managing them successfully, and avoiding harsh lessons like those we learnt in Angola.

Corruption

Angola charges son of ex-president Dos Santos with fraud

- The son of Angola's former president has been charged with fraud relating to a US$500-million transaction out of an account belonging to the central bank.
- José Filomeno dos Santos is the former head of Angola's US$5-billion sovereign wealth fund.
- His passport has been seized and he is forbidden from leaving the country.[9]

– Reuters report

Case study 3.2: Nigeria's MTN fiasco

MTN is a successful multinational South African company that started operations in Nigeria in 2001. As of December 2019,[10] MTN Nigeria had declared an annual service revenue of US$3.3-billion and had EBITDA (earnings before interest, taxes, depreciation and amortisation) of US$1.7-billion with profits of US$805-million. All these indicators showed healthy double-digit growth from the prior year. In 2019, MTN Nigeria had 64.3 million subscribers in Nigeria, which was a 10.5% increase from the previous year, representing a 43% market share. Being a truly African multinational company, MTN has operations in 21 countries across Africa and the Middle East.[11] No-one would expect such a seasoned entity to battle any major threats on this continent, let alone in Nigeria, where it enjoys phenomenal growth and market share.

The picture wasn't always so rosy. Just four years earlier, in 2015, MTN Nigeria was fined a hefty US$5.2-billion[12] by the telecoms watchdog, the Nigerian Communications Commission (NCC). To put that significant penalty into context, it represented around half of MTN's annual revenue at the time, and exceeded its 2014 group profits. In the context of Nigeria, the fee was about a quarter of the 2015 national budget.

What brought about such a strong penalty? The slap was a result of MTN's alleged late disconnection of 5.1 million unregistered SIM cards between August and September 2014. The Nigerian government maintained that failure to register these cards may have enabled attacks by Boko Haram, the Islamist movement that had been terrorising the country's northeast for six years. After many in-court and out-of-court negotiations, as well as intervention by the Nigerian and South African governments, the fine was reduced to US$1.7-billion, with MTN given an option to list its shares on the Nigerian Stock Exchange.[13]

In August 2018, MTN Nigeria was in the headlines again. This time, the Central Bank of Nigeria instructed MTN to repatriate US$8.1-billion – money it believed MTN had taken out of the country with what it called "irregular capital importation certificates issued over the period 2007 to 2015". MTN Nigeria was accused jointly with four banks believed to have assisted it in these illegal transactions. The banks were all multinationals: Standard Chartered PLC, Stanbic IBTC Bank PLC, Citibank and Diamond Bank PLC.

After going through senate hearings, the charges were dropped.

A month after this accusation, MTN Nigeria was fined a tax bill of US$2-billion. After intense deliberations in court, a nominal fee was agreed on with the revenue authorities for US$53-million.[14]

To the outsider, none of this seemingly vindictive behaviour makes any sense. MTN was seen as the government's major service provider, and a significant contributor to the economy. To understand the picture better, one must consider that the relationship between South Africa and Nigeria, the largest economies on the continent, has always been frosty – largely as a result of their rivalry, but also due to the xenophobic attacks on foreigners in South Africa, which have targeted Nigerian nationals, and have been happening more frequently in the last decade. Lastly, president Muhammadu Buhari, who came into power in Nigeria in May 2015, had a strong mandate from his voters to aggressively deal with the Boko Haram terrorist problem. For MTN, these factors created the perfect storm: a toxic interplay of politics, law, taxation, trade and international relations.

In the last few years, it would seem that the company has been on the mend. But the fines they paid as well as the legislative costs they incurred obviously have had a significant impact on their business, both financially and reputationally. It goes to show that threats in the African landscape can be very real for MNCs, even the biggest – and they may need to invest more than they bargained for.

Profile: Rock bottom in Zimbabwe

When you meet Rob Watson for the first time, it's difficult to read him. He's not loud, nor is he sophisticated. He's also not a qualified economist, even though he has an intimate knowledge of the nuts and bolts of economics. He also has a deep business acumen and, as a seasoned entrepreneur, Rob epitomises the businessman who has been able to successfully weather the storm in a pear-shaped economy.

That was something I came to learn long after I first met him in 2001. At that time, I had just joined his company, Chips Computing Services, as an implementation systems analyst for a business management software application called Sage Line 500. As mentioned previously, Chips was the official distributor for business management software solutions, targeting mid- to large-sized companies in Zimbabwe. Sage, the principal, was a listed company on the London Stock Exchange, with a regional office in South Africa.

At that time, Zimbabwe was beginning to feel the impact of having a US$9.7-billion GDP with a "growth" of -0.5%. And things in Zimbabwe were about to get worse. Between 2001 and 2008, according to IMF figures, Zimbabwe's real GDP shrank by -0.5% to -16.3% per annum. Zimbabwe had hit rock bottom. There was a massive exodus of the white community, especially farmers, as their land was invaded. The economic slump resulted in a parallel shortage of foreign currency and fuel. Inflation hit the roof, escalating to 231,000,000% in 2008. If you were white, owned a business that required foreign currency and had a farm, the last place you wanted to be found, dead or alive, was Zimbabwe.

Rob ticked all those boxes as he also had shares in a family-owned farm. But even under these dire circumstances, Chips, under Rob's leadership, was establishing itself as one of the leading Sage distributors in the region. Rob was consistently named one of the top three Sage distributors in US dollars for the AAMEA (Africa, Australasia, Middle

East and Africa) region. In November 2017, Chips won the reseller awards.

If you ask Rob, he will tell you that this remarkable achievement was possible because he stuck to the basics of doing business. While others in Zimbabwe were misled and tried to exploit the economic downturn, Rob maintained credibility by operating the organisation prudently and sturdily. Even though I worked for Rob for many years and now have more than 17 years of additional experience to draw on, when I interviewed him recently, I discovered more about how he managed to Rumble in the Jungle.

Rob reminisces about how most accounting applications in Zimbabwe were unable to cope with the increase of digits brought about by hyperinflation. These applications had been developed in stable markets, where the number of digits needed was easily accommodated in the normal database fields. With inflation escalating to ridiculous levels, it was necessary for the regional distributor to get the software vendor to customise the application. Since Zimbabwe was a small player in the global software market, most US- or Europe-based vendors were reluctant to do this, mainly because the effort outweighed the return on investment.

As fortune would have it, at the time, the SME product team for SagePastel, which was the software-development team for Sage, was located next door to Rob's South African office. The proximity and Rob's credibility both played a part in helping him get the necessary changes made to the application. And once this fix was available, demand escalated, despite the country's recession. Zimbabwean companies needed working accounting software to manage costs in their businesses, and SagePastel stood out because of its local relevance and available support. This basic solution to a basic problem is what allowed Chips to survive at a time when there were no guarantees.

Rob also began to realise that the longer he stayed in Zimbabwe's harsh operating environment, the more he picked up on additional handles that allowed him to sustain his business. As companies were closing, his competition was decreasing, which further opened up the market for his business. And because of its sound educational system, Zimbabwe had developed a healthy base of skilled Sage consultants who were being "exported" to South Africa. By remaining in the eye of the Zimbabwean storm, Rob slowly but surely began to capitalise on these opportunities.

As time went on, it became evident that a quick response was needed under Zimbabwe's particular (and peculiar!) market conditions: clients needed an application flexible enough to accommodate Zimbabwe's 51 different taxes and the ever-changing legislation affecting payroll and accounting software. An example of this is fiscalisation, which uses technology to connect to retailers' point-of-sale machines for the immediate reporting of tax. The accuracy of the accounting software supplied to these machines was critical as discrepancies could result in tax penalties for the retailers. Another example is pricing, or how transactions were captured on applications. The existence of a thriving black market had encouraged people to dabble between invoicing in US dollars and the local currency, which created absolute chaos in the market. In these instances, the "first-mover advantage" was critical for suppliers like Rob.

Long-term vs short-term investments were another thing Rob had to grapple with. In a stable economy, it's easier to plan your investments as you have reasonable forecasts of the future. With Zimbabwe's political and economic landscape being totally unpredictable, such planning was almost impossible.

A case in point is when, in the last quarter of 2017, the new finance minister of Zimbabwe, Professor Mthuli Ncube, activated certain new taxes on electronic payments. These were controversial, and retailers like pharmacies fought back, protesting that they would not sell to the public unless they received hard cash – which was very difficult to get. Not only was their business revenue affected as a result, but pharmacy clients, who are often patients in dire need of treatment, suffered indirectly. Those retailers who made a plan not only acquired additional business, but also gained customer loyalty for having stuck around. In such an environment, speed of reaction and adaptability are absolutely critical.

Rob's story shows how a combination of opportunity, basic business acumen, networking and maintaining credibility with clients, stakeholders and principals all add up to allow a business to weather a particularly African storm. And he notes three other factors that contributed to his success in dealing with the unexpected threats:

- Having a good bank
- Employing a good accountant
- Retaining a good lawyer!

Case study 3.3: The best medicine

One cannot talk about doing business in Africa and not confront the elephant in the room: the topic of racism and xenophobia.

By default, racism in Africa means white undermining black. Wikipedia defines racism as "prejudice, discrimination, or antagonism directed against someone of a different race based on the belief that one's own race is superior". Xenophobia is defined as "the fear or hatred of anything that is perceived as being foreign or strange".

I would argue that both are as bad as each other, and both are clearly still a reality in Africa. But things are changing. In many organisations, unconscious bias training is becoming a normal experience, and our younger generations can be seen to be increasingly accepting of interracial and intercultural spaces and relationships.

In recent years, I have attended a number of shows by Trevor Noah – the world-renowned South African comedian and host of *The Daily Show* in the US. As a person of mixed race, he brings South African audiences in jam-packed auditoriums to tears – black, white, Indian and coloured people laughing together as he mocks racism in this racially polarised country.

Trevor Noah perfectly illustrates how humour can heal the wounds of the past and build on the common interest and the goodwill for which South Africans are renowned. Until we transition to a truly free and non-discriminatory society, humour provides one way of coping with the less-than-perfect realities of the present.

Today's generation will have to continue to persevere against these significant threats to their freedom, but I believe – and hope – that we are heading in the right direction. Certainly, they remain factors for consideration for any MNCs doing business in Africa.

Questions to ask yourself

- What are your greatest threats as you expand in the African market?
- What have you done to mitigate the risks?
- Are you prepared to adapt rapidly when new threats arise?

GRAB OPPORTUNITIES

"A roaring lion kills no prey."
African proverb

The fight: A bee and a bear

Ali was in great form, and by the fifth round, Foreman was getting tired, his previously powerful blows turning to glances and taps. After another three rounds, a combination of Ali's rope-a-dope technique and his strategic "dancing" in the ring had worn out the formidable giant. Sensing an opportunity, Ali grabbed it with both hands.

[In] the eighth, like "a bee harassing a bear", as one Times reporter wrote, Ali peeled himself

off the ropes and unleashed a barrage of quick punches that seemed to bewilder the exhausted Foreman. A hard left and chopping right caused the champ's weary legs to buckle, and he plopped down on the mat. The referee counted him out with just two seconds to go in the round.[1]

A few tactical blows were enough to lay Foreman out on the canvas. Foreman managed to rise to one knee, but before he had got to his feet, referee Zack Clayton had signalled the end of the fight.

Round 7: Nothing ventured, nothing gained

In my years spent searching for and capitalising on opportunities on the African continent, I have realised that many MNCs miss opportunities that are right in front of them – sometimes due to ineptitude, but often due to procrastination and overthinking. Having been a senior executive for a leading global audit and consulting firm, I well understand the importance of proper due diligence before undertaking any major venture, but this should not negate the spirit of entrepreneurial thinking, the need to "seize the moment". The nature of opportunity is such that there is always a measure of risk – and with too much research, debate or thinking, you may just miss your chance.

Through the company I work for, I am a non-executive director for the British Chamber of Business in South Africa and chairman of the American Chamber of Commerce in South Africa, which represent MNCs from the UK and the US operating in Africa. Such is the extent of the latter's influence that the estimated collective turnover of the MNCs it represented in 2019 was equivalent to 10% of South Africa's GDP. The annual board strategy session was looming, which normally would have been held over a weekend at a prime resort... but then Covid-19 struck. The team I led was responsible for working closely with the Chamber's chairman and CEO in putting together our strategy – and they asked me to facilitate a strategy session online.

With the benefit of hindsight, this may seem quite straightforward, but at the time it was completely unknown, and the reputational risks of failing the online assignment were high. To start with, the board had close to 15 members, each of whom was a CEO or equivalent of an internationally listed company.

There were an additional 15 sub-committee leaders (also C-suite in calibre), creating an audience of roughly 30 people who would each have to log in from various locations. The strategy session had to run on Microsoft Teams, with advanced online collaborative tools that allowed for the capturing of ideas and notes.

It felt like the blind leading the blind; neither we nor the client had done a virtual facilitation before. Furthermore, with the Chamber being an NPO with limited funds, we were doing this pro bono – although I did see our involvement as a strategic opportunity to bring our capability to key decision-makers in the marketplace.

Although I initially resisted taking on the assignment, a coordinated effort led to tremendous success. After three virtual strategy sessions spread over three weeks with pre- and post-meetings, the client signed off on the project. Our reward came a few months later. A foreign government trade representative who also sat on the board was so impressed that she asked us to run another programme – one that involved more than 200 delegates from 50 countries in Africa and the Middle East, as well as the US. This one was billable – testament to the benefits of playing the long game.

As it turned out, our participation in both of those assignments has opened up yet more opportunities, and we have gone on to successfully run programmes for clients in the Middle East and Russia – all from Africa. In less than two years, our successful pro bono project has secured at least US$500,000 worth of business, with the same amount in the pipeline.

I strongly believe that the opportunities in Africa arise from converting challenges and problems into something positive. Indeed, nothing ventured, nothing gained.

"I've wrestled with alligators, I've tussled with a whale, I have handcuffed lightning and thrown thunder into jail."
Muhammad Ali

Personal experience: African Millennial

I was born in 1977, so I just missed being a Millennial, also identified as Generation Y. My wife just made it

– so I definitely don't want to be misquoted as being "anti-Millennial"! Still, this is a generation that has a bit of a, shall we say, "reputation". Mention the M-word in the corporate environment, and the older generation tunes out, while the younger generation begins to preen. I like to think that those in between them, like myself, take the best aspects of both.

In terms of numbers, Millennials have become a significant group in business – and they will continue to change things, often for the better, in the coming decades. African Millennials have incredible opportunities before them. Covid-19 has forced us to recognise that 4IR is no longer an option but a necessity. This is a generation at home with new technologies that will enable Africa to scale up and prosper. At the same time, if this generation turns towards imported goods rather than resolving local problems, there is the lurking danger that (as in the past) Africa becomes bloated as a destination for consumables rather than an industrial originator. We must instead aim to be able to produce and process goods for export.

An inheritance of centuries of colonial indoctrination, historical stigma and prejudice is one of the most cynical consequences of colonialism and apartheid – and getting rid of these is key to Africa's future success. There is a great need for Africa to write its own narrative because, as the African proverb says, "Until lions tell their own stories, tales of the hunt shall always glorify the hunter." With the knowledge of where their predecessors erred, they know what not to repeat – Millennials are well positioned to tell the lion's story.

In the present context, it is clear that Millennials are going to have a greater responsibility than they have ever imagined. Perhaps sooner than they care to admit, our current elders will need to hand over the leadership baton, and it is incumbent upon us all to create a sense of real and exciting anticipation for those following in our footsteps. In time, Millennials will in turn impart their knowledge and experience to the upcoming Generation Z. My three young sons are growing up as Zs.

For them and their peers, my hope is that Africa will have a critical mass of leaders who share an inspiring vision for the continent. Driven by pride in this vibrant, colourful continent, and led by a mass movement for change supported by new thinking for the future, it is my dream that inspired, educated leaders deliver a new age of prosperity for Africa.

A renaissance – not a revolution.

Round 8: African money

I used to love reading *Forbes Africa*, especially when Chris Bishop was the editor. In his introductions to African success stories, he'd always lay a firm foundation before unpacking the details. His book *Africa's Billionaires*, alongside titles like *Africa's Greatest Entrepreneurs* by Moky Makura and *Africa Is Open For Business* by Victor Kgomoeswana, presents stories of the many people who are successfully creating wealth in Africa.

In my lifetime, I have worked for two global multi-nationals. One was a world leader in business management software; the other was one of the leading professional services firms in auditing and consulting. Through my experience, I have come to realise that wealth does not choose those to make poor or those to make rich. Rather, it is those who already possess wealth who are better able to make more.

Why is it that Africa seems to have such a challenge in creating wealth? The poor in Africa are not at fault. To a large extent, the poor in Africa are poor because there are not enough entrepreneurs and successful businesspeople creating sustainable wealth.

In *Capitalist Nigger*, Chika Onyeani claims that most of the solutions for Africa's problems reside within its people. I agree. In my own view, whether we are physically on the continent or abroad, if we remain alert to opportunity, we can all be part of the solution.

Case study 4.1: Making it happen in Kenya

Kenya has established itself as the tech hub not only of East Africa but of the entire African continent. Coming out of the country, technology-driven innovations like M-Pesa and a number of others have helped establish this position.

In 2010, the software company I was with needed to conduct a feasibility study on whether we should open a branch office in Kenya as part of our "grow Africa" strategy. With our offering of business solutions for small, medium and large corporations, we seemed to be lagging behind, as some of our competitors such as SAP, Microsoft and Oracle had already established offices there.

Although I was leading the relevant business unit, I was sceptical about opening an office in Kenya. I was not confident that we would get the ROI, especially considering the significant investment required.

Fortunately, one of our managers volunteered to base herself in Kenya, and came back with enough on-the-ground intel to help us make a decision. After much deliberation and research, we decided to open the Kenyan office. While there was still significant risk, we realised timing was crucial – if we did not act immediately, we would lose a key spot in a strategic market.

Kenya's technology-savvy environment indicated that the market was positioned to grow exponentially, and one key indicator gave insight into Kenya's particular propensity for technology adoption: a report published during that period showed that 11% of global mobile phone users regularly made or received payments on their phones.[2] The mobile payment usage in Africa's two largest economies, Nigeria and South Africa, was 13% and 29% respectively. But Kenya knocked the ball out of the park with a phenomenal mobile payment usage of 68% – confirmation that we were right to open our Nairobi office.

A few years later, we were gratified by tangible proof of our ROI as some product lines saw more than 100% year-on-year growth in US dollars. Now that was an opportunity I was glad we grabbed!

The technology hub
The rise of innovation hubs supporting start-ups in Africa
The proliferation of innovation centres to support start-ups on the continent is driven by rising mobile and internet penetration, and Kenya is leading the way.[3]
– Financial Mail headline

Case study 4.2: The Alibaba factor

From an African perspective, it seems that when we talk of Africa-China relationships, they are usually to the Chinese advantage. The common narrative highlights how Africa has been abused by the stronger economic and political power as China, a leading global economy, takes advantage of Africa by capitalising on its natural commodities in exchange for cheaper loans. The story goes that when the Chinese lead infrastructure projects in Africa, the quality of the roads, bridges and buildings they create is mediocre; and they prefer to use their own nationals rather than developing local skills.

Some degree of responsibility for this situation lies with our African leaders: the Chinese sell their offerings based on what we Africans pay, and they deliver no more than we demand. Consider that many of the leading technology companies from Europe or the US, such as Apple, have their components manufactured in China – and I am yet to hear people complain that their original iPhone is substandard! African leadership must take ownership of the Africa-China relationship and ensure that it is mutually beneficial.

Jack Ma, who founded Alibaba in 1999, has become one of the world's richest people, renowned not only as a Chinese innovator but also as an astute adopter of trends. The e-commerce platform he built is now stiff competition to established models like eBay and PayPal.[4]

After his first trip to Africa in 2017, Ma was excited by the opportunities he saw. He is quoted as saying, "If we all work together to support entrepreneurs, then Africa will become a hub of innovation and growth, the global leader we know it can be."

In June 2018, Ma took young entrepreneurs from 14 African countries (Botswana, Ethiopia, Nigeria, Ghana, Kenya, Rwanda, South Africa, Algeria,

Cameroon, Chad, Egypt, Tunisia, Uganda and Zambia) through his Alibaba Business School[5] to develop their skills. During the Covid-19 pandemic, in association with Ethiopian Airlines, Ma supplied Africa with at least 5.4 million face masks and other items of personal protective equipment (PPE).

Ma's motive for this support is closely tied with his original mission: for his e-commerce platform to flourish among Africa's growing population. Enabling platforms in other countries strengthens a worldwide network of small to medium enterprises and "grows the pie" for all, rather than spurring a global fight over a single pie. The more open, platform-based businesses there are in the world, the more opportunities there will be for all players (including Alibaba), and the more partnerships will be possible in the long term.

In his dealing with Africa, Jack Ma is applying the same principles that allowed him to successfully nurture a billion-dollar business in China's emerging market. He knows that the future of his African business is only as good as its people, so he has a stake in their wellbeing. By investing in education and health in Africa, he is proving his commitment and cultivating the soil for future rewards.

Profile: Business in Egoli, City of Gold

Established out of the 1880s gold rush, Johannesburg was nicknamed in the local Setswana vernacular as Egoli, meaning the "City of Gold". As much as the name highlights opportunity, it also suggests the polarising wealth that would soon follow. Today, the thriving city probably has the strongest GDP of any city in Africa.

When I first relocated to Johannesburg with my wife and first-born son, then only a baby, we rented an apartment in the northern suburbs. On evenings when the baby became restless, I would take him out onto the balcony and show him the glittering skyline of the city in the distance, and I'd whisper, "Egoli, Egoli". Somehow, that comforted us both.

As beautiful as the city looked against the night sky, it was by then no longer a commercial hub. Due to crime and administrative challenges, most big companies and residents had already relocated from the Johannesburg city centre to the northern satellite of Sandton, which had become the new CBD. As commerce and residents fled to safer locations, a vacuum was created in the older city, and criminals filled the void.

Over the years, public and private society have tried to rehabilitate the city, and bring back the illustrious years. Following a promise of opportunity, individuals with vision have seen beyond the murkiness and risen to the challenge – similar to the original gold miners of over a century ago, who saw in the highveld wilderness the promise of gold and a better life.

One such an individual is Okai-Farayi Chiyanga. I became acquainted with him through a mutual friend, who believed that the talks I did on "Winning Business in Africa" aligned with the phenomenal work Farayi was doing with young entrepreneurs and creative artists in the Johannesburg city centre.

When I was invited to meet him at his office in Eloff Street – not the most savoury of places – I had to put on a brave face. The building I was directed to was on a corner opposite a building that once housed the renowned Dorkay nightclub – where Nelson and Winnie Mandela first met in the club's heyday. Neglected over time, today it's a run-down mess of cheap accommodation and shabby office space. But at No. 1 Eloff Street, the Formation Building has been renovated, with businesses premises on the ground and mezzanine floor, and residential accommodation above. It is here that Farayi has started what one may call an Africa-themed shared office space and incubator, creating a platform that allows start-up entrepreneurs to leverage ideas and abilities off one another. In connecting like-minded individuals (entrepreneurs, NPOs and artists, among others) in a mutually supportive environment, The Formation HUB counters the prevalence of start-up failures in Africa.

Farayi was born in Canada to parents who were originally from Africa. When he was six, his parents returned to Zimbabwe, where he grew up to become a doctor. Clearly, Farayi has always had a passion for helping people. He points out that his training and the challenges he faced as a trauma doctor in Zimbabwe when the economy was at its worst taught him life lessons that helped him shape his vision of The Formation HUB. With a Ghanaian mother, a Zimbabwean father and a South African wife, it is understandable that Farayi's vision is truly pan-African. He sees his work as a calling, which he cannot abrogate on principle, especially with his roots so deeply embedded in African soil.

Having been introduced to the facility through a family friend who was in the property business,

Farayi prides himself on having self-funded the hub, rather than borrowing capital. With time, The Formation HUB has become more than just a place for entrepreneurs to work; it's become a true intersection of artists and businesspeople. The Formation HUB has had its challenges, but Farayi's dream has already made an impact. I hope that, by harnessing Africa's diversity, natural wealth and human capital, it will grow to fulfil its vision of helping Africa's future business owners to capitalise on the opportunities ahead.

Questions to ask yourself

- What opportunities do you see on the African continent?
- What is stopping you from grabbing them?
- How can you prepare yourself to be ready for the next opportunity that arises?

LESSON 5
APPLY RELENTLESS DRIVE AND DETERMINATION

"The elephant does not limp when walking on thorns."
African proverb

The fight: No ordinary mortal

No-one could underestimate George Foreman. His strength was undeniable – he could throw seemingly limitless punches in close succession, each one capable of dazing and destroying. No ordinary opponent could withstand such a barrage.

Ali was no ordinary mortal. On a mission, he believed from God himself, Ali withstood Foreman's offence. Instead of wilting before the storm, like a great sequoia Ali bent, leaning back into the loose ring ropes, avoiding the worst of Foreman's fury, gritting his teeth and bearing that which he could not dodge.[1]

Years later, Foreman later told Ali's biographer, Thomas Hauser: "What I remember most about the fight was, I went out and hit Muhammad with the hardest shot to the body I ever delivered to any opponent... Anybody else in the world would have crumbled. Muhammad cringed."

For the spectators who witnessed it, there was something otherworldly about Ali's determination. Without it, Ali would not have survived eight rounds of iron-fisted pummelling. In Ali, Foreman's immense strength met a profound inner resolve. As Foreman would later say, "I could see it hurt. And then he looked at me. He had that look in his eyes, like he was saying, 'I'm not going to let you hurt me.'"[2]

It was a trait that won him the respect and awe of the entire world.

Round 9: How to finish a marathon

To survive in the African business jungle, you need raw grit and determination; that is the intangible layer that lines the gut of anyone who wants to grow their business in Africa.

Another famous boxer, Mike Tyson, said, "Everyone has a plan until they get punched in the mouth." Many of us will know the panic that ensues when your plan is unexpectedly torpedoed. Whether it is government legislation, political crisis, war, social unrest, weather or sabotage, the punches can feel relentless. It is not how badly you fall but how quickly you get up that will determine your success.

In sports, stories of determination abound, and that of marathon-athlete John Stephen Akhwari is another source of inspiration. In 1968, he competed on behalf of his country, Tanzania, in the Mexico Olympics. The story goes that he started the marathon as planned, but somehow injured his leg. It required first aid and he had to exit the race to be treated. By then, he had fallen far behind the other runners, but he insisted on continuing. At the stadium, the other runners were applauded as they crossed the finishing line, and the winners were interviewed by the media. Everybody had assumed that the last runner had come in.

As the crowd was packing up to go, someone noticed John Akhwari limping into the stadium. One can only imagine his pain, but he soldiered on, determined to make it across the finishing line. Everyone turned to watch…

He crossed the finish line and was immediately surrounded by a swarm of reporters keen to find out what had gone wrong, and why he had continued despite his injury. His response made history: "My country did not send me 5,000 miles to start the race – they sent me 5,000 miles to finish the race."

Nothing sums up African determination better than that.

> *"If my mind can conceive it, and my heart can believe it – then I can achieve it."*
> **Muhammad Ali**

Case study 5.1: The Econet story

Econet Global is a privately held pan-African telecommunications, technology and renewable-energies group focused on digitally connecting customers in the 28 markets, mostly in sub-Saharan

Africa,[3] where it has operations and investments. It was founded in Zimbabwe by its current chairman, Strive Masiyiwa (mentioned in Lesson 3), and has an estimated turnover of more than US$3-billion. Over the years, Econet has developed a converged offering of products and services spanning mobile telephony, fibre infrastructure, media broadcasting, financial services (fintech), e-commerce, Internet of Things (IoT) and renewable energy. Through these, Econet has transformed the societies in which it operates by connecting people and improving their lives.

Econet's story is one of a successful African-born multinational business that has capitalised on the needs and opportunities of Africa. Originating in my home country of Zimbabwe, it's a story I've seen play out from the beginning. In *Africa's Billionaires*,[4] Chris Bishop notes that Strive Masiyiwa is worthy of the nickname "Bill Gates of Africa", not just because of his business success but also due to his philanthropic initiatives, which have seen thousands of university scholarships being offered worldwide, and millions of lives saved as a result of his investment in the health sector, among other industries.

But Strive's success did not happen overnight. Having qualified abroad as an electrical engineer, he returned to Zimbabwe to give back. It was in 1993, while he was working for the national telecoms company, that he developed the entrepreneurial vision to establish the first mobile network in Zimbabwe. This was a massive opportunity: he knew that mobile communications was the next frontier, though not even five countries in Africa had built such networks. In most countries, state-owned fixed-line operators were providing a sub-standard service.

Given the positive impact it would have for the people of Zimbabwe, one would imagine the regulatory body would have easily granted him the licence. But as the saying goes, "If wishes were horses, beggars would ride." For the next five years, Strive was embroiled in a court battle with the government as he fought to get his mobile licence. Resistance came from high up – from president Robert Mugabe himself. Strive had to draw on every inner resource, including his strength as a Christian, as everything around him – finances, businesses and family – came under attack. At the time, he had a successful construction company with a number of government contracts, but as soon as he appealed to the courts, he found his government contracts cancelled. His income source was crippled, and he eventually had to sell the business.

But amid all this turmoil and persecution, Strive had the support of a large population of Zimbabweans – and I know this because I was one of them. In the court papers, it was clear the state wanted to maintain a monopoly of the telecoms industry. Strive's legal team countered that, by doing so, the government was restricting freedom of expression and undermining the constitutional right of freedom of speech.

While the five-year-long court battle raged, the government issued mobile service-provider licences to Netone, which was largely owned by the government, and Telecel, which had local and international shareholders. Strive persevered, and in 1998, while he was praying alone in a room overseas, he got a telephone call from a colleague. The Supreme Court had announced its verdict in his favour: he had finally been granted the licence.

This landmark ruling is regarded as one of the milestones in opening up African telecommunications to private capital and investment, which has led to rapid growth, expansion and transformation of the communications landscape across the continent. Today, Econet is Zimbabwe's market leader over Netone and Telecel.

Over the past few years, Strive has devoted his time to mentoring the next generation of African entrepreneurs through his Facebook page, which has an ever-growing number of followers – more than four million – from across the continent. Facebook has identified his page as having the most engaged following of any business leader in the world.

The African landscape is strewn with the carcasses of entrepreneurial ideas that fell to bureaucratic attack. But Strive's story may provide inspiration and hope for the success stories of tomorrow.

Profile: Making it happen in South African townships

In Cosmo City, a township north of Johannesburg, two impressive Millennials have grown a leadership programme for teenagers. In 2016, Irvin Dzakatira and Honest Ncube created a programme called Shape Your Destiny Youth (SYDY) through the NPO Boys and Girls Youth Africa. The 10-week programme targets teenagers in their final year of high school to teach them leadership skills. The three main components of the course are Identity, Relationship and Basic Business Principles.

In the programme's first four years of existence, Honest and Irvin impacted the lives of at least 150 teenagers in their community, using their own money and that of well-wishers. I became involved with their team when they asked me to give talks for their leadership course. It's always exciting to motivate and encourage the next generation, as it reminds me of how helpful it was for me when I was encouraged at that age.

Irvin comes from a broken home and has lived most of his life in South Africa. His parents were separated, and he grew up in poverty exacerbated by family challenges. With a talent for mathematics and science, he began helping others after leaving school by tutoring high-school kids in his community. Irvin has been unable to fund full-time university studies, but has been able to complete a correspondence degree in applied mathematics and the sciences through UNISA. His vision is to one day build a leadership tutorial institution for young people, with a pan-African footprint.

Honest came from a more sheltered background, and was exposed to different southern African cultures from an early age. He realised he had a gift for building relationships and "putting things together" in order to help people. After meeting Irvin through a mutual colleague at the Cosmo Community Centre, they developed the SYDY model.

At the time of going to print, the pandemic and other factors had significantly disrupted the SYDY operations – yet I still wanted to tell their story because of the impact they have had on both their community, and on me. As foreigners in South Africa, they have already faced the challenges of xenophobia and a lack of government support, among others, and I believe they will conquer the new obstacles in their way with similar fortitude and resilience. They have always been motivated by passion and the validation of seeing young people reach for their dreams. The commitment, sacrifice and tenacity of these young men is truly humbling.

Questions to ask yourself

- How determined are you to succeed in the African market?
- How much are you willing to sacrifice?
- What obstacles and setbacks might you need to overcome in the short-, medium- and long-term?

CONCLUSION
AFRICAN HORIZON

"If you want to go quickly, go alone.
If you want to go far, go together."
African proverb

For Ali, what started with morning jogs among the people on the streets of Kinshasa ended with the triumph of a nation. The underdog had won – seemingly against all odds – and the celebrating went on for days. In such a joyous atmosphere, it seemed as if even the heavens were in on the deal:

An hour after the fight, the sky opened. The long-threatened storm had finally come, flooding the arena with three inches of water in a matter of hours. That did little to stop the celebrations, with the Africans celebrating their own burgeoning glory as much as Ali's iconic win.[1]

What made Muhammad Ali such an outstanding exponent of his sport?

To begin with, I would say that he knew how to connect with people. He had wit and a way with words – but he also had heart, and that is something that the people of Kinshasa responded to. In the ring itself, he could never be called one of boxing's hardest punchers; it has been noted that more than a third of his professional contests lasted their full scheduled duration. Nor was he remarkable in terms of height or weight; the younger Foreman had the advantage there. As sports broadcaster Alan Hahn notes, "What distinguished Ali from other competitors was his speed, agility, footwork and athleticism – it was said he was a heavyweight who moved like a lightweight."[2]

And finally, he had a strategy that paid off. Ali worked with his strengths to become the greatest – and surely the most celebrated – boxer in history. I see a lot of parallels with Africa in George Plimpton's summation of the aftermath of the event:

I think it was the sort of joyous reaction that comes with seeing something that suggests all things are possible: the triumph of the underdog, the comeback from hard times and exile, the victory of an outspoken nature over a sullen disposition, the prevailing of intelligence over raw power, the success of physical grace, the ascendance of age over youth, and especially the confounding of the experts. Moreover, the victory assuaged the guilty feelings of those who remembered the theft of Ali's career. It was good to watch and hear about, whichever fighter one supported. Indeed, one of the prevailing stories the morning after the fight was that never had so many large bets been handed over so cheerfully to their winners.[3]

If we take Ali's example into the world of business, we will turn perceived challenges into strengths and come out on top. We have nothing to lose.

In summary

Based on the iconic Muhammad Ali vs George Foreman fight in 1974, here are the five lessons that can be applied to doing business in Africa:

Lesson 1: Understand the territory

With 54 countries on the continent, Africa is a cauldron of culture, politics and people. It is important to understand the DNA of the African territory in which you are hoping to operate.

Lesson 2: Innovate

Thinking out of the box is key, especially in Africa's emerging markets, where the conditions (and the rules) are different to those in the West.

Lesson 3: Know your threats

The PESTLE environment in Africa is unique and complex compared to other continents. It is imperative to align your strategy accordingly to threats, especially those beyond your control.

Lesson 4: Grab opportunities

If you delay, you lose! When looking for opportunity, research is important – but action is even more important.

Lesson 5: Apply relentless drive and determination

No pain, no gain. Drive and determination are crucial in this challenging market. After all, Africa is not for sissies!

I hope this book has provided some inspiration and some food for thought.

Sala kahle (Zulu for "Stay well")

ENDNOTES & RESOURCES

Prologue

1 "How Muhammad Ali won 'Rumble in the Jungle' with rope-a-dope, video analysis and no sex" by Jeremy Wilson, in *Daily Telegraph*, 5 June 2016; telegraph.co.uk/boxing/2016/06/05/how-muhammad-ali-won-rumble-in-the-jungle-with-rope-a-dope-video
2 *Dictatorland* by Paul Kenyon (Head of Zeus, 2018)
3 *Muhammad Ali: His Life and Times* by Thomas Hauser (Simon & Schuster, 1991)

Introduction

1 "Predatory Behaviour: Lions Hunting", Lion Alert (8 January 2020); lionalert.org/predatory-behaviour
2 "Spotted Hyena: Interesting Facts", Altina Wildlife Park; altinawildlife.com/spotted-hyena
3 "Amazing Facts About Africa's Wild Dogs – Dynasties of Survivors" by Elize Loubser, Wilderness Safaris (9 April 2021); wilderness-safaris.com/blog/posts/amazing-facts-about-africa-s-wild-dogs-dynasties-of-survivors
4 "The pecking order of the world's population is soon to change", *The Economist* (14 July 2022); economist.com/graphic-detail/2022/07/14/the-pecking-order-of-the-worlds-population-is-soon-to-change
5 "Tracking Africa's Progress in Figures" by the African Development Bank Group (2014); afdb.org/fileadmin/uploads/afdb/Documents/Publications/Tracking_Africa's_Progress_in_Figures.pdf

6 "Boosting Resilience Through Social Protection" by the Office of the Chief Economist in the World Bank Africa Region (13 April 2022); worldbank.org/en/publication/africa-pulse

Lesson 1: Understand the territory

1 "Muhammad Ali Wins Rumble in the Jungle", This Day in History; history.com/this-day-in-history/muhammad-ali-wins-the-rumble-in-the-jungle

2 "Muhammad Ali's Greatest Fight: George Foreman and the Rumble in the Jungle" by Jonathan Snowden, *Bleacher Report* (4 June 2016); bleacherreport.com/articles/1919959-muhammad-alis-greatest-fight-george-foreman-and-the-rumble-in-the-jungle

3 Ibid.

4 Ibid.

5 There is some dispute about what constitutes an individual country. I use the UN's stated number of 54 independent countries.

6 "Mapped: Visualising the True Size of Africa" by Jeff Desjardins, *Visual Capitalist* (19 February 2020); visualcapitalist.com/map-true-size-of-africa

7 "The Land Area of the Continents", Enchanted Learning; enchantedlearning.com/geography/continents/Land.shtml

8 "Official and Spoken Languages of African Countries", One World Nations Online; nationsonline.org/oneworld/african_languages.htm

9 "Native North American Languages", The Language Gulper; languagesgulper.com/eng/Northamer.html

10 "Indigenous Languages of South America", MustGo; mustgo.com/worldlanguages/indigenous-languages-of-south-america

11 Extracted and adapted from "Continent: Africa", The Joshua Project; joshuaproject.net/continents

12 "What Is M-Pesa?", Vodafone; vodafone.com/what-we-do/services/m-pesa

13 Ibid.

14 "Why Vodacom M-Pesa has flopped in SA", Fin24 (9 May 2016); fin24.com/Tech/Companies/why-vodacom-m-pesa-has-flopped-in-sa-20160509

15 "Five reasons M-Pesa failed in South Africa" by XN Iraki, *The Standard* (2016); standardmedia.co.ke/article/2000201831/five-reasons-m-pesa-failed-in-south-africa

16 "How Zimbabwe's economy was brought to the brink of collapse" by Tony Hawkins and David Pilling, *Financial Times* (19 November 2017); ft.com/content/5fe10fea-cd13-11e7-b781-794ce08b24dc

17 "Hyper Inflation in Zimbabwe" by Tejvan Pettinger, *Economics Help* (13 November 2019); economicshelp.org/blog/390/inflation/hyper-inflation-in-zimbabwe

18 "Zimbabwe's Black Market for Foreign Exchange" by Albert Makochekanwa, in the *Working Paper Series* of the Department of Economics at the University of Pretoria (July 2007); repository.up.ac.za/bitstream/handle/2263/4396/Makochekanwa_Zimbabwes(2007).pdf

19 "Zimbabwe's inflation rate surges to 231,000,000%" by Chris McGreal, *The Guardian* (9 October 2008); theguardian.com/world/2008/oct/09/zimbabwe

20 Tweet by @Yuesie on Zimbabwe's 2018 election, sourced from ewn.co.za/live/LIVE-BLOG-Zimbabwe-holds-historic-election (30 July 2018)

21 "Land Audit Report" (Version 2) by the South African Department of Rural Development & Land Reform (November 2017); gov.za/sites/default/files/gcis_document/201802/landauditreport13feb2018.pdf

22 "South Africa's youth continues to bear the burden of unemployment" by the Department of Statistics South Africa (1 June 2022); statssa.gov.za/?p=15407

23 "Fact Sheet: Founding the Right to Health" by Section27 (May 2019); section27.org.za/wp-content/uploads/2019/05/2019-IEJ-S27-Health-Fact-Sheet.pdf

24 "Global Innovation Index 2021: Tracking Innovation Through the Covid-19 Crisis" (14th Edition) by the World Intellectual Property Organization (2021); wipo.int/edocs/pubdocs/en/wipo_pub_gii_2021.pdf

25 The YMCA was founded in London on 6 June 1844 by Sir George Williams, who aimed to put Christian principles into practice by developing a healthy "body, mind and spirit"; en.wikipedia.org/wiki/YMCA

Lesson 2: Innovate

1 "Muhammad Ali (American boxer)" by Thomas Hauser, in Britannica; britannica.com/biography/Muhammad-Ali-boxer

2 "Muhammad Ali Wins Rumble in the Jungle", This Day in History; history.com/this-day-in-history/muhammad-ali-wins-the-rumble-in-the-jungle

3 "Crafting Strategy" by Henry Mintzberg, in *Harvard*

Business Review (July 1987); hbr.org/1987/07/crafting-strategy

4 *The Innovator's Dilemma: When New Technologies Cause Great Firms To Fail* by Clayton Christensen (Harvard Business Review Press, 1997)

5 "Global Employment Trends for Youth 2020: Africa", by the International LAbour Organization; ilo.org/wcmsp5/groups/public/---dgreports/---dcomm/documents/briefingnote/wcms_737670.pdf

6 "'Youth are starved of opportunities', say experts ahead of Youth Day" by Michelle Banda, *Daily Maverick* (16 June 2022); dailymaverick.co.za/article/2022-06-16-youth-are-starved-of-opportunities-say-experts-ahead-of-youth-day

7 Graph adapted from africaprogresspanel.org

8 *Nuts & Bolts – Strengthening Africa's Innovation And Entrepreneurship Ecosystems* by McLean Sibanda (Tracey Macdonald Publishers, 2021)

9 World Bank 2010 figures

10 "Rwanda – Contribution of travel and tourism to GDP in current prices"; knoema.com/atlas/Rwanda/topics/Tourism/Travel-and-Tourism-Total-Contribution-to-GDP/Contribution-of-travel-and-tourism-to-GDP

11 Rwanda GDP Growth Rate 1961-2022; macrotrends.net/countries/RWA/rwanda/gdp-growth-rate

12 "Basketball Africa League 2020 – Who will grab the last three tickets?" (17 December 2019); fiba.basketball/africaleague/2020/qualifiers/news/basketball-africa-league-2020-who-will-grab-the-last-three-tickets

13 "Zipline mastered medical drone delivery in Africa – now it's coming to the US" by Amy Farley, *Fast Company*

(10 March 2020); fastcompany.com/90457727/zipline-most-innovative-companies-2020

14 "How Nick Leeson caused the collapse of Barings Bank" by Paul Monthe, *Next Finance* (February 2007); next-finance.net/How-Nick-Leeson-caused-the

Lesson 3: Know your threats

1 "Muhammad Ali's Greatest Fight: George Foreman and the Rumble in the Jungle" by Jonathan Snowden, *Bleacher Report* (4 June 2016); bleacherreport.com/articles/1919959-muhammad-alis-greatest-fight-george-foreman-and-the-rumble-in-the-jungle

2 "The Influence of institutional factors on MNCs' triple bottom-line reporting: A focus on African emerging markets (AEMs)" by Boris Urban and Rutendo Hwindingwi, *International Journal of Emerging Markets*, Vol 11(4) pp 497-513 (September 2016)

3 The methodology used was based on the National Leadership Index created by the Center for Public Leadership at the Harvard Kennedy School

4 "Global Leadership Index", World Economic Forum, based on the Survey on the Global Agenda (2015), from weforum.org. The WEF no longer produces this report, though its annual "Global Risk Report" conveys similar information.

5 World Bank figures; data.worldbank.org/indicator/NY.GDP.MKTP.CD?locations=AO

6 Ibid.

7 "FMCG in Africa: Sector report for the period 2000-2013", KPMG (2015)

8 "Corruption Perceptions Index", Transparency International (2006); transparency.org/en/cpi/2006

9 "Angola charges son of ex-president dos Santos with fraud" by Reuters, CNBC (27 March 2018)

10 MTN Nigeria FY19 results; mtn.com

11 mtn.com

12 "What MTN's woes say about doing business in Nigeria" by Clementine Wallop, *KYC360* (14 March 2016)

13 "FACTBOX-South Africa's MTN faces challenges in largest market Nigeria" by Reuters staff (10 September 2018)

14 "Nigeria backs down on MTN's $2bn tax demand" by Alan Burkitt-Gray, *Capacity* (13 January 2020)

Lesson 4: Grab opportunities

1 "Muhammad Ali Wins Rumble in the Jungle", This Day in History; history.com/this-day-in-history/muhammad-ali-wins-the-rumble-in-the-jungle

2 Pew Research Center (2013)

3 This 2018 headline highlights the tech progress in Kenya. "The rise of innovation hubs supporting start-ups in Africa" by Michael Schmidt, *Financial Mail* (19 July 2018)

4 "Tech Giants Are Engaged in a New Scramble for Africa" by Howard French, *World Politics Review* (18 December 2019)

5 "Chinese internet giant Alibaba shares its plans for Africa" by Monique Vanek, CNBC (9 July 2018)

Lesson 5: Apply relentless drive and determination

1 "Muhammad Ali's Greatest Fight: George Foreman and the Rumble in the Jungle" by Jonathan Snowden, *Bleacher Report* (4 June 2016); bleacherreport.com/articles/1919959-muhammad-alis-greatest-fight-george-foreman-and-the-rumble-in-the-jungle

2 Ibid. Quotes originally from *Muhammad Ali: His Life and Times* by Thomas Hauser (Simon & Schuster, 1991)

3 econetafrica.com

4 *Africa's Billionaires – Inspirational Stories From The Continent's Wealthiest People* by Chris Bishop (Penguin Random House, 2017)

Conclusion

1 "Muhammad Ali's Greatest Fight: George Foreman and the Rumble in the Jungle" by Jonathan Snowden, *Bleacher Report* (4 June 2016); bleacherreport.com/articles/1919959-muhammad-alis-greatest-fight-george-foreman-and-the-rumble-in-the-jungle

2 "What made Muhammad Ali 'The Greatest' in the ring?" by Alan Hahn, *Life Hacker* (6 June 2016)

3 "Return of the big bopper" by George Plimpton, *Sports Illustrated* (23 December 1974)

ACKNOWLEDGMENTS

First and foremost, I would like to thank my lovely and affectionate wife P, and my sons Joshua, Nathan and Arnold, for their continual support during the process of writing this book.

My father Stephen Kotsai Hwindingwi and my late mother Mabel Sekai Hwindingwi will always be the bedrock of my success in life.

I would also like to thank the multitude of people who have contributed to the completion of this project, specifically Reg Wessels, who helped shape and write the manuscript, and my publisher, Tim Richman, along with his team, for being so patient and accommodating.

And finally, to two late mentors of mine who left an indelible mark: Moosa Kasimonje and Sajeed Sacranie. Rest well knowing that your efforts were not in vain.